UNION INTERNATIONALE DES SCIENCES PRÉHISTORIQUES ET PROTOHISTORIQUES
INTERNATIONAL UNION FOR PREHISTORIC AND PROTOHISTORIC SCIENCES

PROCEEDINGS OF THE XV WORLD CONGRESS (LISBON, 4-9 SEPTEMBER 2006)
ACTES DU XV CONGRÈS MONDIAL (LISBONNE, 4-9 SEPTEMBRE 2006)

Series Editor: Luiz Oosterbeek

VOL. 18

C44

The Early Neolithic in the Iberian Peninsula
Regional and transregional components

Le Néolithique ancien dans la Péninsule Ibérique
Les éléments regionaux et transregionaux

Edited by

Mariana Diniz

BAR International Series 1857
2008

Published in 2016 by
BAR Publishing, Oxford

BAR International Series 1857

Proceedings of the XV World Congress of the International Union for Prehistoric and
Protohistoric Sciences / Actes du XV Congrès Mondial de l'Union Internationale des Sciences
Préhistoriques et Protohistoriques
*The Early Neolithic in the Iberian Peninsula / Le Néolithique ancien dans la Péninsule Ibérique ,Vol. 18,
Section C44*

ISBN 978 1 4073 0340 6

Outgoing President: Vítor Oliveira Jorge
Outgoing Secretary General: Jean Bourgeois
Congress Secretary General: Luiz Oosterbeek (Series Editor)
Incoming President: Pedro Ignacio Shmitz
Incoming Secretary General: Luiz Oosterbeek

Contacts : Secretary of U.I.S.P.P. – International Union for Prehistoric and Protohistoric Sciences
Instituto Politécnico de Tomar, Av. Dr. Cândido Madureira 13, 2300 TOMAR
Email: uispp@ipt.pt   www.uispp.ipt.pt

BAR Publishing is the trading name of British Archaeological Reports (Oxford) Ltd.
British Archaeological Reports was first incorporated in 1974 to publish the BAR
Series, International and British. In 1992 Hadrian Books Ltd became part of the BAR
group. This volume was originally published by Archaeopress in conjunction with
British Archaeological Reports (Oxford) Ltd / Hadrian Books Ltd, the Series principal
publisher, in 2008. This present volume is published by BAR Publishing, 2016.

Printed in England

BAR
PUBLISHING

BAR titles are available from:

BAR Publishing
122 Banbury Rd, Oxford, OX2 7BP, UK
EMAIL   info@barpublishing.com
PHONE   +44 (0)1865 310431
FAX   +44 (0)1865 316916
www.barpublishing.com

TABLE OF CONTENTS

LIST OF FIGURES

LIST OF TABLES

PREFACE

Mariana DINIZ

Centro de Arqueologia da Universidade de Lisboa – UNIARQ

m.diniz@fl.ul.pt

It's clear today that Europe neolithisation can no longer be explain as a single model process. Both demic and cultural diffusion processes were operating side by side creating a cultural patchwork where regional and transregional elements set together to create something new.

This settled a great metaphor for contemporaneous world – with people, resources and technologies being transfer from different areas – a small step towards a global economy since exogenous elements soon became crucial in Iberian Neolithic landscapes.

In Iberian Peninsula, like in other parts of Europe, domesticates, both plant and animals, pottery and polished stone tools are clearly transregional, with a exogenous origin and younger chronologies as we travel West.

However, the way in which this components were, or were not, used mixed with other and adapt to particular environmental and social conditions were regional or even local.

In this way, monolithic explanations seem to have failed. Neolithisation process was not a "big wave" that covered the whole continent, but demic diffusion alongside with acculturation processes seems responsible for Iberian Early Neolithic.

Geo-cultural regions emerged or kept their personalities and we still can find internal differences in Iberian archaeological record, between Mediterranean and Atlantic, littoral and interior groups.

In about one thousand years – from the middle sixth to the middle fifth millennium cal BC Iberian landscapes change from a hunter-gatherer territory to an agro-pastoralist zone. Understanding these dynamics, which affects all aspects of human societies, was the main purpose of this workshop, held in 9 September 2006, in Lisbon.

Special attention was given to:

– methodological issues concerning both chronological and stratigraphical data (Rojo-Guerra *et al.*; Estrada García *et al.*; Ortega *et al.*);

– social complexity arose from landscape monumentalization and symbolic territorialisation within cardial (Bernabeu Aubán *et al.*), non-cardial (Calado and Rocha), and "megalithic" groups (Clop and Gibaja);

– other non-cardial but still Early Neolithic groups in Inner Iberian archaeological record (Rojo-Guerra *et al.*; Cerrillo Cuenca);

– new data from Central and Southern Portugal Early and Middle Neolithic habitats (Gomes, Neves *et al.*).

Mariana Diniz

Lisbon, 2007

THE PORTALÓN AT CUEVA MAYOR (SIERRA DE ATAPUERCA, SPAIN): A NEW ARCHAEOLOGICAL SEQUENCE

A.I. ORTEGA[1]; L. JUEZ[1]; J.M. CARRETERO[1,2]; J.L. ARSUAGA[2,4]; A. PÉREZ-GONZÁLEZ[3];
M.C. ORTEGA[2]; R. PÉREZ[1]; A. PÉREZ[1]; A.D. RODRÍGUEZ[1]; E. SANTOS[1]; R. GARCÍA[1];
A. GÓMEZ[1]; L. RODRÍGUEZ[1]; M. MARTÍNEZ DE PINILLOS[1] & I. MARTÍNEZ[2]

[1] Laboratorio de Evolución Humana, Departamento Ciencias Históricas y Geografía, Edificio I+D+I,
Plaza de Misael Bañuelos s/n, 09001, Burgos
[2] Centro UCM-ISCIII de Investigación sobre Evolución y Comportamiento Humanos,
c/ Sinesio Delgado, 4. Pabellón 14, 28029 Madrid
[3] Departamento de Geodinámica, Facultad de Ciencias Geológicas,
Universidad Complutense de Madrid, 28040 Madrid
[4] Departamento de Paleontología, Facultad de Ciencias Geológicas,
Universidad Complutense de Madrid, 28040 Madrid
[5] Departamento de Geología, Edificio de Ciencias, Universidad de Alcalá, 28871, Alcalá de Henares, Madrid

Abstract: The site of Portalón at Cueva Mayor, located in the Sierra de Atapuerca (Burgos, Spain), is an important Holocene archaeological site that was excavated in the 70's but from which little has been published. New excavations starting in 2000 have highlighted a deep stratigraphical sequence with human occupations starting in the beginning of the Upper Pleistocene. In this paper, we present for the first time this stratigraphical sequence with a set of radiocarbon datings comprising from 30.000 BP to 2000 BP.
Keywords: Sierra de Atapuerca; Estratigraphy; Radiocarbono datings; Holocene, Upper Pleistocene

Resumo: O sítio de Portalón, Cueva Mayor, situado na Serra de Atapuerca (Burgos, Espanha), é um importante sítio arqueológico do Holoceno, escavado na década de 70, e sobre o qual pouca informação havia sido publicada. Novas escavações, iniciadas em 2000, puseram a descoberto uma longa sequência estratigráfica, com ocupações humanas que remontam ao Pleistoceno Superior. Neste trabalho, apresenta-se pela primeira vez, a sequência estratigráfica, para a qual existe um conjunto de datações por radiocarbono compreendidas entre 30.000 BP e 2000 BP.
Palavras-chave: Serra de Atapuerca; Estratigrafia; Datações de radiocarbono; Holoceno; Pleistoceno Superior

INTRODUCTION AND HISTORICAL FRAME

The Sierra de Atapuerca is located about 15 km to the east of the city of Burgos, on the northeastern edge of the Northern Sub-plateau of the Iberian Penninsula. This geographic location is strategic. The north-south lines of communication that penetrate toward the interior of the Penninsula pass through it, along with those that develop east-west communicating with the basin of the rivers Duero and Ebro.

This sierra encloses an important karst in which the Cueva Mayor-Cueva de Silo cave systems standout (Martín Merino *et al.* 1981). Its entrance is a large chamber known as the "Portalón of Cueva Mayor" where there has been different occupations throughout its recent prehistory (Fig. 1.1).

The first scientific study of Cueva Mayor carried out in the last third of the 18th century (Sampayo and Zuaznávar, 1868), motivated the visit of other researchers who delivered news of the first archaeological remains of the recent prehistory of Portalón (Carballo, 1910), as well as the existence of diverse panels of post-paleolithic art (Breuil, 1913).

In 1966, Francisco Jordá, professor at the University of Salamanca, carried out the first archaeological excavation of Portalón, but his results were never published. In 1972, Geoffrey Clark, a researcher at the University of Arizona, interested in surveying the Upper Paleolithic sites of the Northern Plateau, made two test pits in Portalón; one 2x2 m that yielded altered sediments to a depth of 2 m, and another of 0.5x2 m that revealed an in situ stratigraphy 2.6 m deep (Clark 1979, 94-95; Fig. 1.2). Clark identified three cultural periods in the stratigraphic sequence, attributing the first three levels (1-3) to the Roman period; levels 8 to 20 to different stages of the Bronze Age and levels 21 to 26 to phases of the Neolithic (Clark 1979, 96).

The interesting cultural sequence detected by G. Clark motivated Juan María Apellániz, professor at the University of Deusto, to get involved in Portalón to get a better understanding of occupations of those that he designated as "population of the caverns" (Apellániz, 1983) (Fig. 1.2). The excavation between 1972 and 1983, permitted Apellániz to define a series of cultural levels verifying the presence of medieval and late roman materials (levels I and II), and an important occupation during the Bronze Age (Level III). This level was in turn subdivided into a stratigraphic sequence of the Final Bronze Age dated to between 940 and 1220 ±130 B.C. (Minguez 2004, 50), a rich Middle Bronze Age sequence with chronologies of 1450±50 B.C., and a Late Bronze Age squence dated to 1690 ± 50 B.C. (Apellániz and Domingo 1987, 263).

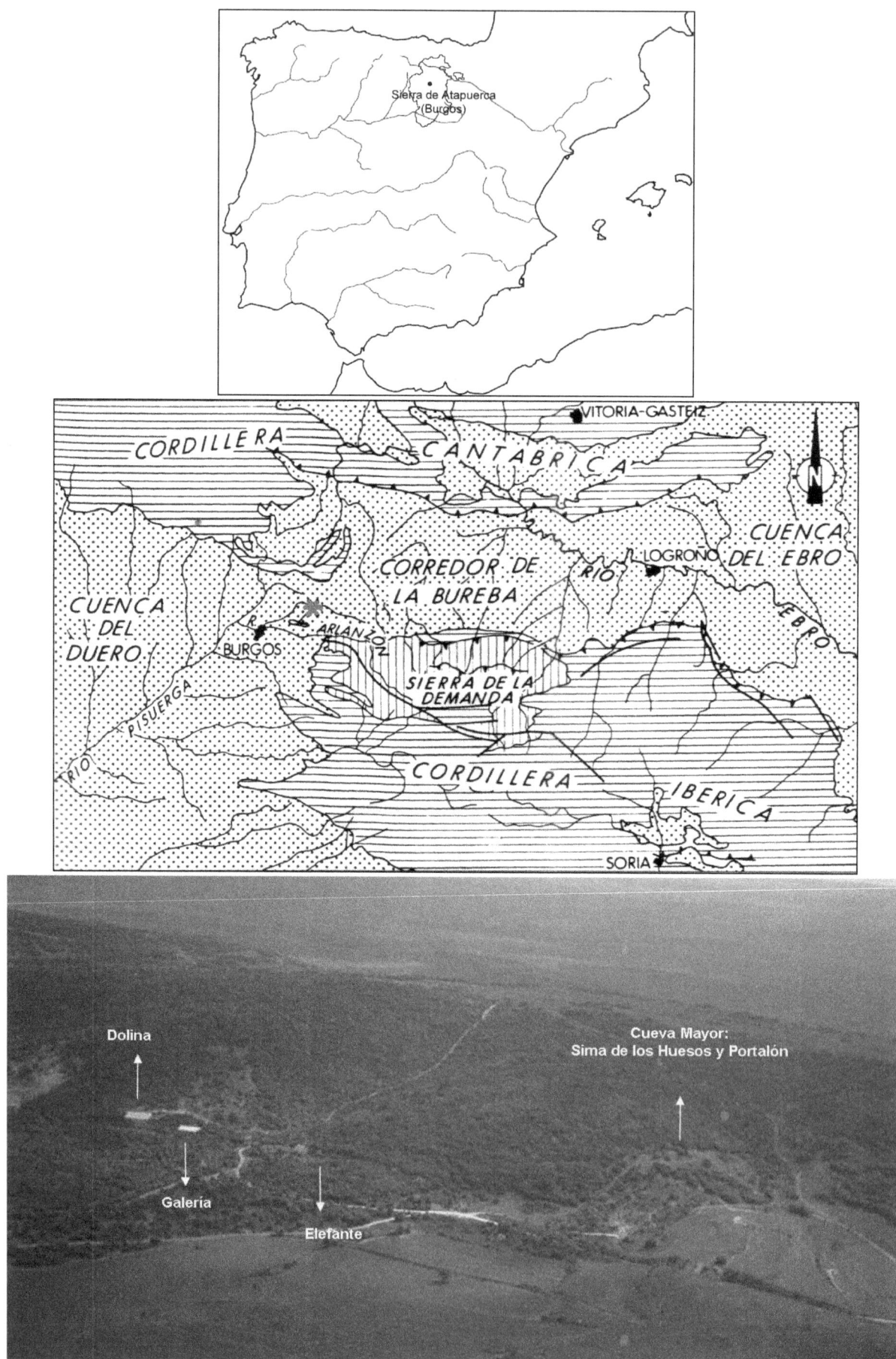

Fig. 1.1. Geographical situation of the Sierra de Atapuerca and the main pleistocene and holocene sites

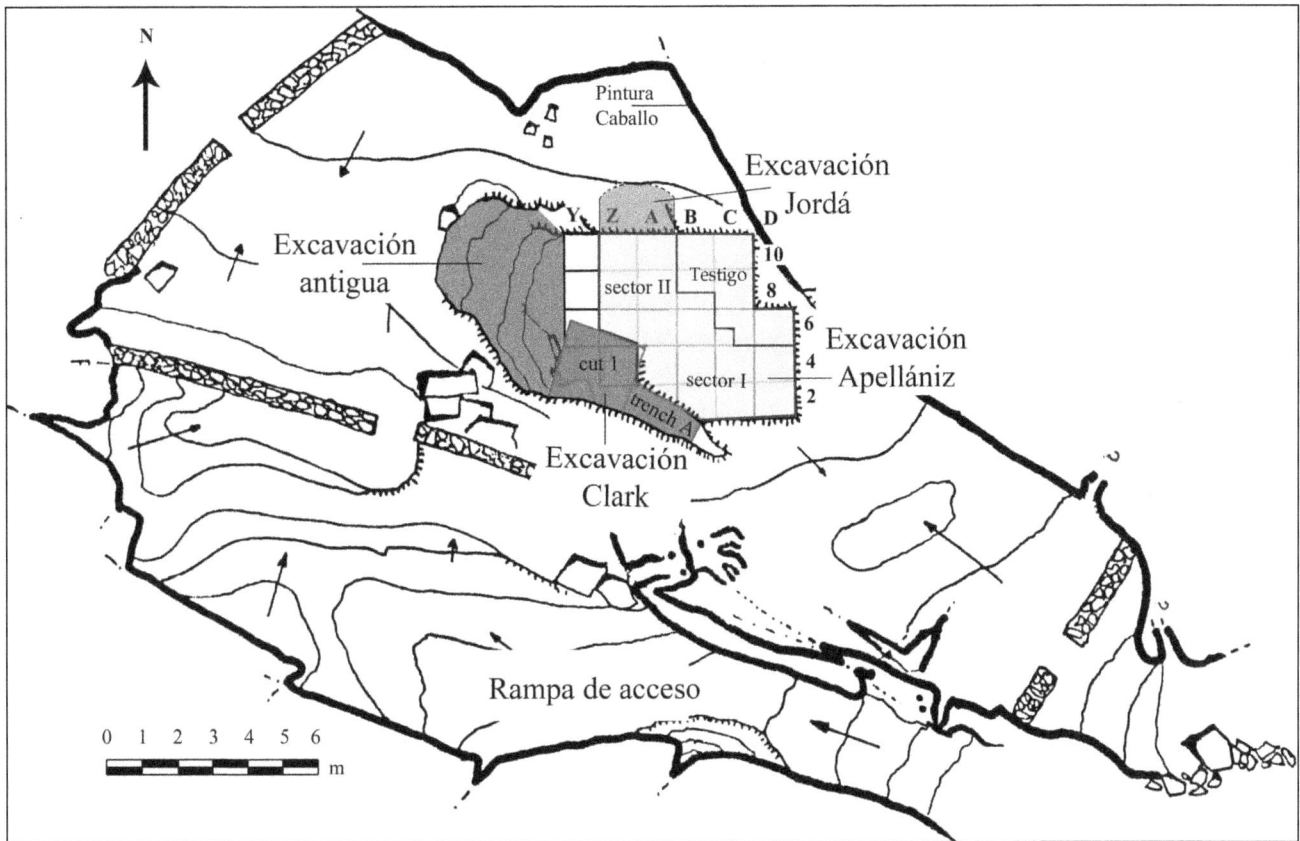

Fig. 1.2. Scaled plan of the Portalón de Cueva Mayor site indicating the different excavations areas

RECENT EXCAVATION OF PORTALÓN (2000-2006)

To a better understanding of the archaeological potential of Portalón we began a new stage of excavations in 2000 within the Proyecto de Investigación de Atapuerca directed by Juan Luis Arsuaga.

Once we delimited the in situ excavation areas of F. Jordá, G. Clark and J.M. Apellániz, we detected the presence of an important excavation in the central part of Portalón, whose authors are currently unknown (Fig. 1.2). From 2001 onward we concentrated all our efforts in delimiting the in situ limits of the site. In order to achieve this, we proceeded to excavate the sediments that filled this earlier excavation, among which we have recovered interesting archaeological material from disturbed contexts (Juez 2005). This intervention consisted of a ditch inclined in an east-west direction of some 2 m in width that gives ways to a hole with an oval cross-section of 2 m in diameter and that, for the moment, has more than 9 m in depth since we still haven't excavated all. Judging by characteristic of this pit we believe it to be a mining intervention.

However, the excavation of the pit has revealed a deep and interesting stratigraphic sequence that was unknown until now.

STRATIGRAPHIC SEQUENCE AND ABSOLUTE CHRONOLOGY

With the current obtained data we have characterized the stratigraphic sequence of Portalón in the North and South profiles and we have divided it into 11 numbered levels from 0 to 10 (Fig. 1.3). The radiocarbon dates (Beta Analytic INC) obtained for the levels of the Portalón sequence are given in Table 1.1.

Tab. 1.1. Radiocarbon dates for Portalón de Cueva Mayor.

Level 0: corresponds to an irregular alteration of the first 15 to 68 cm of the roof of the sequence and composed of a packet by brown muds with organic materials, charcoals, faunal remains and potter's wheel ceramics. It is a partially altered level without absolute dates and with ceramic materials pertaining to the Middle Ages.

Level 1: an ashy layer with disperse charcoals that alternate with dark grey clays forming aggregates, with small limestone klasts, with a maximum thickness of 40 cm. A roman occupation was registered with common ceramics and Terra Sigillata of late-roman and Imperial typologies. There are three radiometric dates for this level: 1980 ± 40 BP, 2040 ± 100 BP and 2050 ± 100 BP.

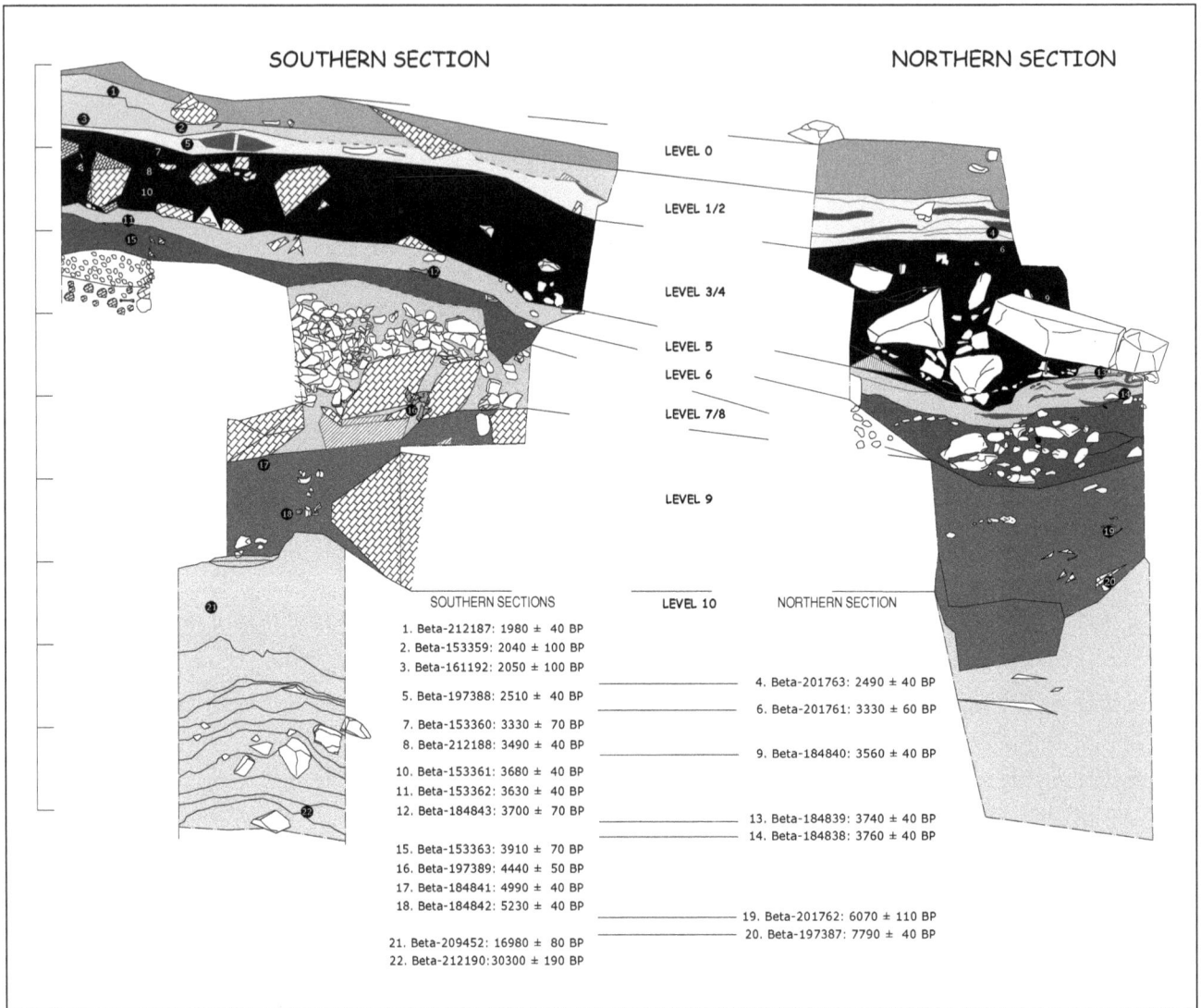

Fig. 1.3. Stratigraphical sequence of the northern and southern profiles from Portalón de Cueva Mayor site indicating the different excavations areas

Level 2: consists of some sediments of anthropic and organic origins where they alter marks with abundant ash and clayey muds of dark tones (7.5YR 7.1), reaching a maximum depth of 30 cm. Hand made ceramics corresponding to the cultural phase of Iron Age I have been recovered in this level, as well as the remains of domestic fauna. In the north profile it is not clear the subdivision between levels 1 and 2. There are two dates for this level, one of 2510 ± 40 BP and the other of 2490 ± 40 BP.

Level 3: consists of a thin collection of dark colored sandy-clayey-muds, of some 16 cm in thickness, where there is plenty organic material with numerous charcoals remains and elements of material cultural, documenting fragments of hand-made ceramic pertaining to the protocogotas cultural phase and abundant faunal remains. The absolute chronology puts this level in the Middle Bronze Age, with two dates of $3330 \pm 60/70$ BP.

Level 4: deep homogeneous packet, of sandy-clayey-muds, of between 70 and 150 cm in thickness, increasing its depth toward the interior of Cueva Mayor. This level is rich in organic and charcoal material, emphasized by the presence of numerous klasts and big limestone blocks originating from the collapse of the walls and roofs of the cavity. Abundant hand-made ceramic fragments are documented in its profiles, as well as pieces of lithic and bone industry, together with the faunal remains. We place the chronology of this level in the Early Bronze Age with four dates that go from 3490 ± 40 BP to 3680 ± 40 BP.

Level 5: level of sandy-clayey-muds of grayish tones (10YR 6/1), with abundant charcoals and ashes in its base. The average depth is of some 35 cm, where there are abundant fragments of handmade ceramics and domestic faunal remains. They show typical dates of the transition of the old Bronze Age to the

6

Chalcolithic that goes from 3630 ± 40 BP and 3760 ± 40 BP. The intervention of Apellániz culminates in this level, documenting a fragment of bell beaker ceramic.

Level 6: level of sandy-clayey-muds of anthropic origin, with abundant organic material and charcoals that have a grayish color. Towards its base, lenses of ash are documented. It presents an average thickness of 30-35 cm. The presence of ceramic and faunal remains are also documented in this level, presenting a date pertaining to the Chalcolithic (3910 ± 70 BP). The intervention of Clark concludes in this unit.

Level 7/8: stand out for their stoney and anthropic attributes, consisting of angular limestone rocks and subangulars rocks without matrix that increase in size with depth. In the base of this level big limestone blocks appear, among which stand out two flat stones of some 70 cm in height by 50 and 65 cm in width respectively. This level presents the form of a tumulus that reaches a maximum height of 200 cm in the Southern Profile, while diminishing in size toward the north. In this structure a relatively abundant amount of human remains are documented, as well as ceramic and faunal fragments. The remains of a large vessel with decorations of pellets, a copper awl and the presence of two goats in anatomical position over the two large flat stones stand out, and have been given a chronology of 4440 ± 50 BP. All this indicates the sepulchral use of this cavity during periods of the chalcolithic.

Level 9: is made up of the final part of the Holocene sequence, composed of a very homogenous packet with anthropic origins, characterized by clayey-sandy-mud sediments with blackish tones, with abundant organic material and rich in charcoals. In this unit sub-angular limestone stones and small calcareous blocks are observed, together with some round stones of quartzite. It has an average depth of 125 cm in its southern profile that increases toward the north at 170 cm. In the base of this large layer the presence of a silo structure is documented with a depth of about 75-80 cm and a diameter of 130 cm that has in turn affected the lower levels (N9a and N10). The documented archaeological record indicates the presence of handmade ceramic fragments and faunal remains, as well as lithic and bone industries. However there is a need to distinguish two very different chronological moments within this level. The superior part of this level is dated at 4990 ± 40 BP, the upper middle level at 5230± 40 BP and the base at 7790 ± 40 BP. An awl of clearly neolithic typology recovered in the northern profile stands out between the elements of material culture and has a chronology of 6070 ± 110 BP. As we see, these dates indicate an occupation situated fully within the Neolithic and another during the Mesolithic period, with a temporal hiatus of 1720 years between both occupations. We still have not detected any remains of ceramics during the visual analysis of the base of level 9 (mesolithic occupation).

Level 9a: a small level of bat guano of between 5 and 8 cm of thickness characterized by sterile muddy-sand sediment for the moment, without absolute dates. It represents the transition between the two documented sedimentary units in Portalón de Cueva Mayor, the superior holocene (N0 a N9) and the inferior pleistocene (N10).

Level 10: This level represents the inferior sedimentary unit that has been in turn divided into 12 numbered sub-levels from P1 to P12. It is characterized by an alternation of angular limestone clasts of more than 1 cm originating from debris flow, containing a muddy-sandy-clay matrix of brownish and orangish tones, inserted between levels of fine sediments which show a near absence of clasts. It presents a visual depth of more than 360 cm, and is abundant in microfaunal remains of cold environments along with a small amount of macrofauna. Small flakes of flint (BP2G) were recovered in the P8 sub-levels. Level 10 belong to the Upper Pleistocene with a date of 16.980 ± 80 BP for the P1 sub-level (around 60 cm of the contact with N9a) and another of 30.300 ± 190 BP for the sub-level P11 (around 335 cm of the same contact).

INTERPRETATION OF THE SEQUENCE OF PORTALON AT CUEVA MAYOR

The archaeological sequence of Portalon has been described in this paper. We can conclude that as the Portalon of Cueva Mayor has been used like habitat place during a long and intense period of time, the stratigraphic sedimentation is continuous and homogenous. Therefore, the correct interpretation of the different occupation levels is very difficult.

The stratigraphic sequence of Portalón presents two principle sedimentary units. The lower unit, identified as N10, has a visible depth of 360 cm, and is characterized by debris flow of clasts with clayey matrix of orangish color, with absence of organic material and with hardly any human intervention. Chronologically it pertains to the last third of the Late Pleistocene and stands out for its paleontological nature and for a weak presence of human activity between 30.000 and 17.000 BP. In the future we may be able to investigate the human settlement of the Plateau during the beginning of the Late Paleolithic.

Above this lower unit, a very clear contact made up of a level of bat guano (N9a), lies the upper unit, with a maximum depth of 630 cm and comprises levels 9 to 0. It is characterized by sedimentary homogeneity and grayish coloring with an abundance of organic material and numerous archaeological remains indicative of highly anthropic levels. In the complete sequence the presence of stones and blocks coming from the roof of the chamber is frequent, being of greater size in the upper unit.

The cultural sequence of this unit indicates the existence of an intense human occupation throughout the Holocene. This occupation began with still very poorly known phases of the Mesolithic and Neolithic (N9). We hardly know the characteristics of these occupations that must have involved nomadic populations in which livestock and agriculture probably complemented the hunting. The chronological results might be related with those of the sites of the immediate surroundings like Galeria del Sílex (Cueva Mayor), Abrigo del Mirador, (also in Sierra de Atapuerca), with the Cascajos (Quintanadueñas) nearby settlement, with Abrigo de Mendandia (Saseta-Treviño) site, Cueva de la Vaquera (Segovia) and Cueva Lóbrega (La Rioja).

The Neolithic sequence culminates in a tumulus structure with funerary characteristics associated with megalithism at the end of the Neolithic and with the Chacolithic world (N8-7), evidenced in Atapuerca and Rubena villages (both in Sierra de Atapuerca).

The continuous sequence of the Bronze Age levels (N6 a N3) represent the best understood moment due to continuous excavation works. The great diversity and quantity of elements of cultural material indicate the importance of the activities developed by the human groups that controlled the surrounding territory. There are several excavated cavities within the Sierra karst complex: Galería del Sílex, Abrigo Mirador and Cueva Ciega at Ibeas de Juarros and Cueva de la Revilla at Atapuerca, are the most outstanding.

Finally, the archaeological sequence completes with the phase of occupation of the proto-historic (N2) and historic epoch (N1 and N0), when the cavity was utilized as sheepfold in order to hold the livestock. This human occupation might be related with the nearby Tritium Autrigonum castrum (Monasterio de Rodilla) and the Roman villae from the Atapuerca village.

CONCLUSIONS

The current archaeological sequence from the Portalón at Cueva Mayor takes on a singular importance due to the scarcity of information on the late Upper Pleistocene, Mesolithic and Neolithic cultural periods in the interior Peninsula and, in particular, in the Northern sub-plateau.

In the Portalón sequence two main sedimentary sequences can be detected. The first one (the lower unit) is correlated with the Upper Pleistocene, which has a very important paleontological record, and a weak human activity presence placed between 30.000 and 17.000 B.P. The second one (the upper unit) is correlated with the Holocene and is characterized by anthropic evidences.

This unit can be divided in two phases, one of them related to the Recent Prehistory, with a continuous settlement in the Mesolithic and Neolithic. It is remarkable the sepulcral character developed during the end of the Neolithic and Chalcolitic, which intensified the Bronze Age occupation. The second cultural phase of Portalón is interpreted as a low use of stable during Proto-historic and Historic periods.

Acknowledgements

We are very grateful to our colleagues and friends from the UCM-ISCIII Research center, LEH of the University of Burgos. Thanks also to Marta Negro curator of Museo de Burgos for providing permission and helpful access to the materials collections in their care. Special thanks go to Ciarán Brewster and Nuria García for their kind revision of the English. This research was supported by the Ministerio de Ciencia y Tecnología, Proyecto nº BOS2003-08938-C03-01. Funding for the field work came from the Junta de Castilla y León and Fundación Atapuerca. Help in the field from the Grupo Espeleológico Edelweiss is essential. Thanks also to excavation Team of Portalón and other Atapuerca sites.

Bibliography

APELLÁNIZ, J.M.; MARCOS, J.L.; DOMINGO, S. (1983): "Informe sobre planteamiento, desarrollo, problemas y futuro del yacimiento arqueológico de "Cueva Mayor de Atapuerca" (Ibeas de Juarros, Burgos)". Diputación Provincial de Burgos. *Inédito.*

APELLÁNIZ, J.M.; DOMINGO, S. (1987): Estudios sobre Atapuerca (Burgos). II Los materiales de superficie del Santuario de la Galería del Sílex. *Cuadernos de Arqueología de Deusto.* Bilbao.

BREUIL, H.; OBERMAIER, H. (1913): "Travaux executés en 1912" *L'Anthropologie.* 24: 5-7.

CARBALLO, J. (1910): "De Espeleología. Recientes descubrimientos prehistóricos y geológicos. Pruebas experimentales de la duración de las pinturas. Glíptica en las cavernas. ¿Astronomía prehistórica?". *Boletín de la Real Sociedad Española de Historia Natural,* 10: 468-481.

CLARK, G. (1979): The North Burgos Archaelogical Survey. An inventory of cultural remains. In The North Burgos Archaelogical Survey: Bronze and Iron Age archaeology on the Meseta del Norte (Province of Burgos, North-Central Spain). In *Anthropological Research Papers*, 19. Arizona State University. Dept. of Antropology, Arizona.

JUEZ, L (2005): Estudio tipológico y contextualización de los materiales cerámicos recuperados en la campaña del año 2000 en el yacimiento del Portalón de Cueva Mayor (Sierra de Atapuerca, Burgos). *Master Tesis.*

MARTÍN, M.A. [*et. al.*] (1981): Estudio de las cavidades de la Zona BU-IV-A (Sierra de Atapuerca). *KAITE, Estudios de Espeleología Burgalesa, 2, 41-76.*

MÍNGUEZ, M. (2005): "Estudios sobre Atapuerca (Burgos): III. Los materiales del Bronce Final de «El Portalón de Cueva Mayor»". *Cuadernos de arqueología,* 20. Excma. diputación de Burgos y Universidad de Deusto.

ORTEGA, A.I., CARRETERO, J.M., JUEZ, L., GARCÍA, R., GÓMEZ, A., RODRÍGUEZ, L., SANTOS, E., PÉREZ, R., ORTEGA, M.C., GUTIÉRREZ-AVELLANISA, A., RUÍZ, M.B., DORADO, M., VALDEOLMILLOS, A., PÉREZ-GONZÁLEZ, A.Y ARSUAGA, J.L. (2004): "Yacimiento del Portalón de Cueva Mayor: revisión de un yacimiento en Cueva", en *IV Congreso de Arqueología Peninsular. Programa y libro de resúmenes,* 67. Universidad do Algarve, Faro.

SAMPAYO, P.Y ZUAZNAVAR, M. (1868): *Descripción con planos de la cueva llamada de Atapuerca.* Burgos.

TORCA L'ARROYU: A NEW HOLOCENE SITE IN THE CENTRE OF ASTURIAS (NORTH OF SPAIN)

Rogelio Estrada GARCÍA[1], Jesús F. JORDÁ PARDO[2], Joan S. MESTRES TORRES[3] and
José Yravedra Sainz de los TERREROS[2]

[1] Arqueólogo Consultor. C/ Río Esva, 7, 1ºA. E-22010 Oviedo (Spain) · rogelio.estrada@teleline.es
[2] Laboratorio de Estudios Paleolíticos. Departamento de Prehistoria y Arqueología. Facultad de Geografía e Historia.
Universidad Nacional de Educación a Distancia. C/ Senda del Rey, 7. E-28040 Madrid (Spain) · jjorda@geo.uned.es
[3] Laboratori de Datació per Radiocarboni. Facultat de Química, 3ª planta. Universitat de Barcelona. C/ Martí i Franqués,
1. E-08028 Barcelona (Spain) · js.mestres@ubu.edu

Abstract: The archaeological site of Torca L'Arroyu was discovered in 2002 during the works of construction of the new net of sewer of Llanera's municipality (province of Asturias, N of Spain). The archaeological deposit is placed inside a small cave and it has provided some ceramic fragments very rolled, two polished lithic pieces, abundant bones of animals consumed by man and charcoals. The archaeological materials and the ^{14}C dates of the bones associated with the ceramics (UBAR-803 4930 ± 70 BP y UBAR-804 4240 ± 60 BP) indicate the existence of an settlement of certain duration that would correspond to the chronological frame of the regional Neolithic. Sites of this chronology are very scanty in the Cantabrian area, therefore, this new deposit will contribute to a better knowledge of the Neolithic in this zone of the Iberian Peninsula.
Key words: geoarchaelogy, radiocarbon, taphonomy, pottery, polish stone, Neolithic, Holocene, Asturias

Résumé: Le gisement holocène de Torca l'Arroyu a été découvert dans 2002 durant les oeuvres de réalisation du réseau d'assainissement de la municipalité de Llanera (Asturias, N de l'Espagne). Le dépôt, situé à l'intérieur d'une petite grotte, a proportionné nombreux fragments céramiques très roulés, deux pièces de pierre polie, nombreux restes osseux d'animaux consommés par l'homme et fragments charbonneux. Les matériels archéologiques et les dates ^{14}C des os associés aux céramiques (UBAR-803 4930±70 BP y UBAR-804 4240±60 BP) nous indiquent l'existence d'un lieu d'occupation de certaine durée que l'on peut attribuer au cadre chronologique du Néolithique régional. Les gisements de cette chronologie sont très peu abondants dans la corniche cantabrique, donc, ce nouveau gisement contribuera à une meilleure connaissance du Néolithique dans cette zone de la Péninsule Ibérique.
Mots clé: geoarchéologie, radiocarbone, taphonomie, céramique, pierre polie, Néolithique, Holocene, Asturias

INTRODUCTION

The site of Torca l'Arroyu is located in the centre of the province of Asturias (UTM: X=270.400, Y=4.810.797, Z=170), in the vicinity of Oviedo (village of La Ponte, parish of Cayés, Council of Llanera) (figure 2.1.A). Its discovery was fortuitous, since it appeared during the works of construction of the new net of sewer of Llanera municipality, in December of 2001. After its find, the construction company stopped the works and asked for the professional services of R.E.G to carry out the archaeological documents of the find. There were previous proceedings to obtain the excavation permit from the Culture Board of the Principado de Asturias. A scanty but interesting collection of ceramic rests stands out among the recuperated materials. There are two polished lithic pieces, a high number of bone rests that belong to macromammals and scanty gastropods.

GEOARCHAEOLOGY: THE CAVITY AND ITS FILLING

The cavity of Torca l'Arroyu is located in the west side of the mesozoical deformed materials of the Oviedo trough in the mesotertiary basin of Asturias. They form the cover of the western extreme of the Central Area of la Cantabric Range (Barnolas y Pujalte, 2004). It is opened in the limestones and marls of the Upper Cretaceous (Cenomanian) which is placed in agreement over the conglomerates, sands and clays of the Albian (IGME, 1973). They appear a few metres below following the slope. At this point, the Cretaceous serie is inclined towards NE with a direction close to N45ºE and a dip of 19º/22º NE. They form the western flank of syncline of Llanera in the NW extreme of the synclinorium of Oviedo-Infiesto.

Geomorphologicaly, the area of Torca l'Arroyu belongs to the morphological division called Longitudinal Depression (Martínez, 1981), it is also called Prelitoral Trough or Intermediate Depression (Martín-Serrano, 1994), which agrees partialy with the unit of relief of the Mesozoical-Tertiary cover (Farias y Marquínez, 1995), units of relief that belongs to the coastal-mesozoical cantabric border, which is located in the NE extreme of the Meridional Hesperian Massif. In this area, the river Nora runs confined within the Cretaceous materials mentioned. It runs from E to W after running through the detritic materials of the Terciary of the Basin of Oviedo; then, the river gets into the Carboniferous limestones of the Naranco hill, more towards the W. Torca l'Arroyu is located in the slope of the right side of the Nora river, which runs among 140 and 150 m. level. The slope ends up in a small plain belonging to the rests of a applanation surface subsequent to the Paleogene, because the river links with the higher levels of the deposit of that

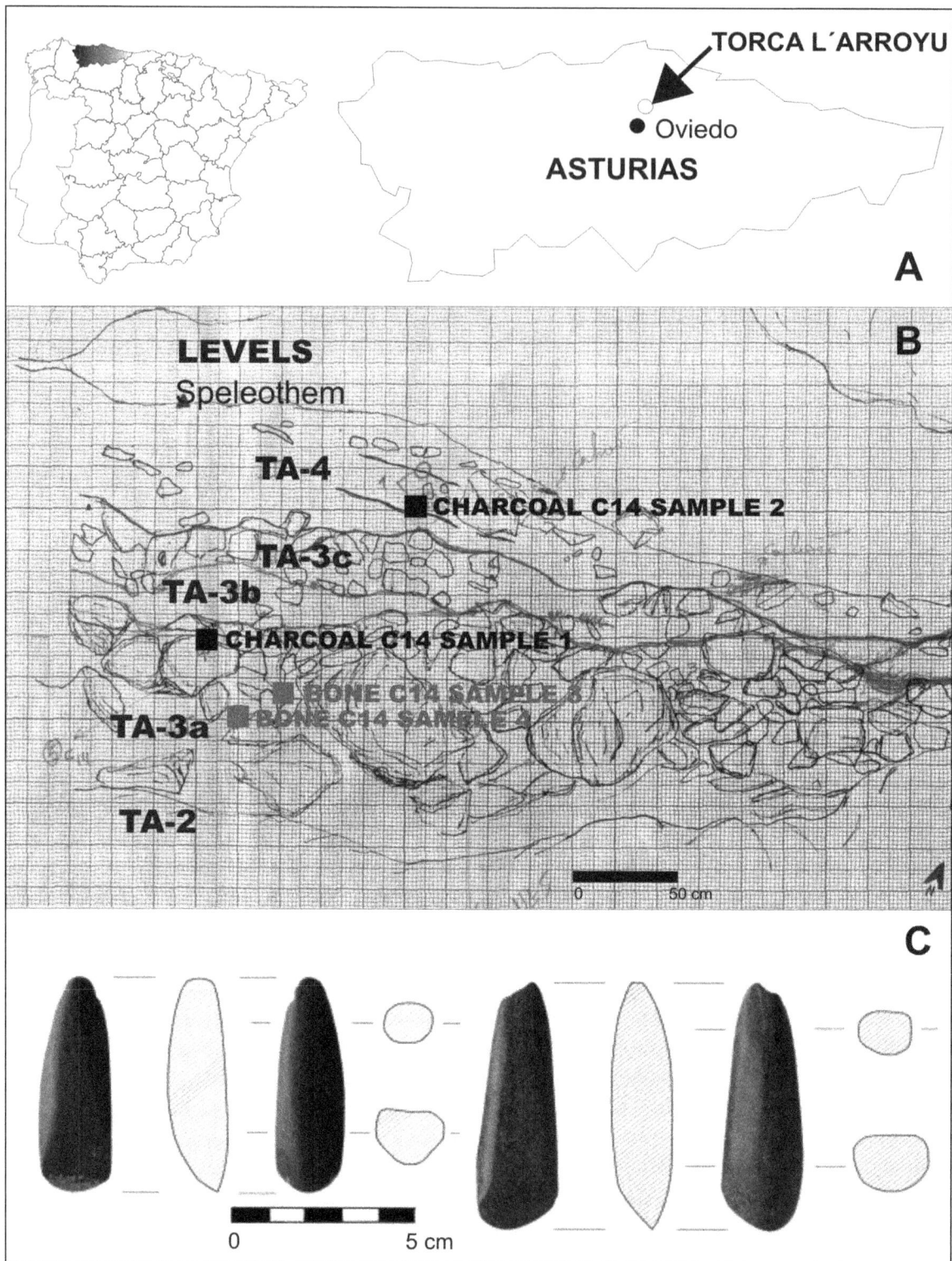

Fig. 2.1. A: Geographical location of Torca l'Arroyu. B: Stratigraphical scheme with indication of ^{14}C samples. C: Polished lithic materials of Torca l'Arroyu

chronology belonging to the Tertiary Basin of Oviedo, and, it is previous to the confinement of the Quaternary fluvial net.

The made gap cut partialy a karstic cavity partialy filled. It is expanded in an alternation of sandy limestones and marls where the first ones prevail. They appear into banks of tabular geometry of metric and high power. We do not have the cenital extreme of the cave. It was wiped out by the construction works on the slope where it was discovered. The access to the outside would be probably in the missing area. The opening would be blinded and would be a collapse sinkhole (*torca*) where the partial filling took place through a deposit formed by a cone of thick and thin detritic materials crowned by a speleotheme. The different stratigraphic sections that can be seen in the gap have allowed to obtain a complete lithostatigraphic sequence from the deposit affected by the works. The base of the sequence lays on the limestones and marls mentioned, which are karstified with an irregular pre-depositonal surface where a threshold area stands out. It is situated, aproximately, in the vertical of the disappeared cenital entrance. This ledge determines the geometry of the deposit; so that two sediment areas can be distinguished. In one of them, the material transport shows a NE direction, and in the other, a S direction. This one is worse controlled due to record disappearance. From wall to ceiling the sequence is composed of the following lithostratigraphic units (figure 2.1.B):

– Unit TA-1: 40 visible cm of clays and yellow sandy marls with small stones of authoctonous lime rounded by alteration (centil: 1 cm), with a high content in carbonates, with irregular geometry, they fill the karstic palaeotopography of the cavity soil. Sterile.

– Unit TA-2: 8-10 cm of dark brown clays with stones of authoctonous lime rounded by alteration (centil: 1 cm), they are very scanty and with a low content in carbonates. It contains scanty rests of mammals and gastropods together with fragments of carbonized organic matter. Its contact is net with the previous materials and its geometry is lenticular, it is getting lost toward the proximal extreme of the deposit. It presents a strong depositional inclination towards NE, it is shaped by the paleotopography of the cavity.

– Unit TA-3. It is composed of three subunits or levels from wall to ceiling:

   o Subunit TA-3a: 60cm – 1 m (in the W profile) of clast-supported conglomerate formed by blocks and pebbles of authoctonous lime (centil 1 m) It's lower contact is net and its geometry is lenticular. It is getting thin towards the proximal extreme of the deposit, it shows a marked depositional dip towards NE. Two lithic polished tools, decorated ceramic fragments and bone rests (sampled for C14) come from those deposits.

   o Subunit TA-3b: 30 cm (in N profile) of brown clays, very plastic, scanty carbonated, with lenticular geometry (maximun lateral extension: 2 m) and inclined arrangement similar to the previous level. They contain many fragments of carbonized organic matter, some bone rests and some specimens of gastropods non-troglophilus. Samples of some charcoals were taken for its radiocarbonic date.

   o Subunit TA-3c: 30-40 cm of clast-supported conglo-merate with scanty matrix, more plentiful at the base. It is formed by boulders and pebbles of authoctonous lime, angular (centil: 30 cm), which include frag-ments of speleothemes that have come off the ceiling

of the cavity , and limy plaquets of 30 cm of maximal dimension and 4 cm of thickness. Both, towards the proximate extreme and towards the distant one, this subunit joints the TA-3a, so that the big clayish lentil remains in the centre. It contains rests of carbonized organic matter and bone rests.

– Unit TA-4: 50-75 cm of very dark brown clays that are arranged parally to the previous subunit. It has a well marked limit due to the lithological difference; however, a discontinuity in the sediment process cannot be seen. This unit shows some internal arrangement outlined by two levels of black organic matter and by the arrangement of authoctonous lime plaquets (centil: 30 cm). They are slightly overlapped parally to the depositional surface, which is configured by some levels with a certain order. Both levels present a remarkable lateral continuity, so that they can be seen in the different cuts. Its depositional inclination is towards NE, the same that is outlined by the alignment of plaquets. They contain bone rests, specimens of non-troglophilus gastropods and fragments of undecorated ceramic.

– Unit TA- 5: 2-10 cm of stalagmite cover that embraces rounded pebbles (centil: 20 cm) and seals the whole detitric deposit that lays below; as a result, there is an inclined crust towards the inside of the cavity with direction N-NE on the surface. It contains non-troglofilus gastropods and bone rests.

THE RECUPERATED MATERIALS

Polished lithic materials

The only recuperated lithic materials (unit TA-3a) are two polished lithic pieces (figure 2.1.C) of a small size made out of amphibolite (length: 69,53 mm and 62,07; mesial width: 19,79 mm and 18,94 mm; mesial thickness: 16,30 mm and 16,02 mm). They present a trapezoidal form that tends to a triangular and lengthened one; a thick profile, a rectangular rounded oval section and a curved thick edge with a very marked asymmetric profile, both pieces are shaped by a bevel (Eiroa *et al.*, 1999). The polishing of the bevel belonging to the bigger piece matches with the one of the ventral side of the piece. It does not show a marked wearing due to use. On the contrary, the bevel of the smaller one shows an oval surface produced by the wearing due to use. It presents a slight inflection with the polishing of its ventral side; besides, it can be appreciated a wearing on its edge, which is also marked by an inflection on the surface of the bevel. There is a concave wearing, lengthened in its back area, which is produced by friction with a cylindrical object. Its heels are pyramidal with a rounded vertex and do not shows percussion marks; the heel of the smaller piece has two lateral notches that are perpendicular to the longitudinal axis (figure 2.1.C.1), probably, related to the handling system, while the one of the bigger piece is affected by a small fracture with a loss of lithic material (figure

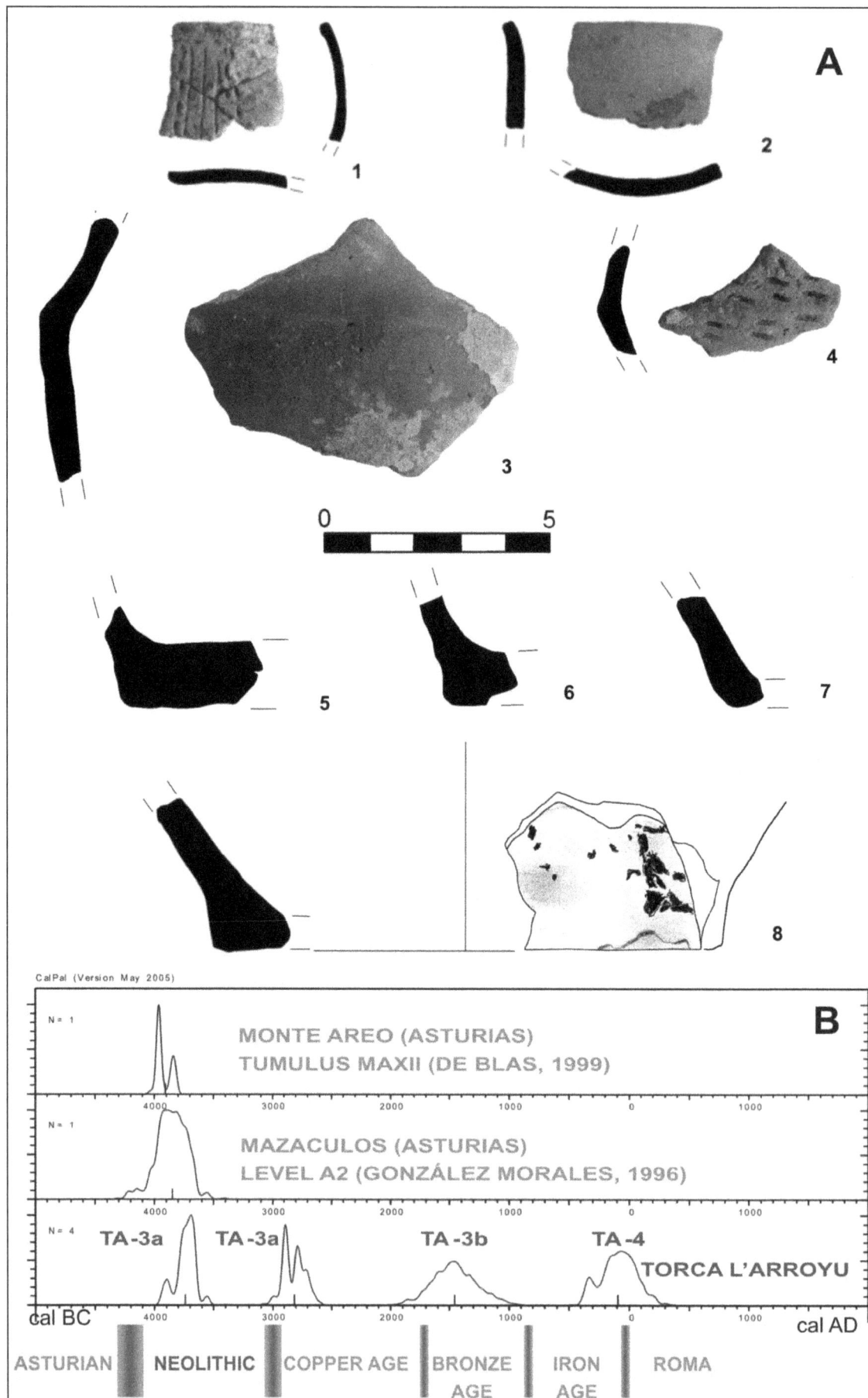

Fig. 2.2. A: Pottery of Torca l'Arroyu. B: Calibrated ^{14}C dates, regional parallels and chronology

2.1.C.2). In relation to their typology, both pieces present the usual characteristics of the chisels (Eiroa *et al.*, 1999), tools used to carve the wood nicely. From our point of view, its more correct denomination would be firmer chisel, because these ones are used to carve wood while the chisels are used to work the stone and the metal. Both lack of percussion prints on the heels, so that they might have been used with handle. This would be proved by the notches that the smaller one has on the heel. Besides, this piece evidences clear signs of use because two types of wearing on its bevel can be appreciated. The bigger one does not show notches on the heel, which is partially fractured, nor clear prints of use, since the ventral and bevel surfaces seems to belong to the making process.

Pottery

The ceramic materials of Torca L'Arroyu form a small collection that is composed of an amount of 68 fragments. All of them are handmade, 61 of them were recuperated in the unit TA-3, five fragments, in the unit TA-4, and two fragments, in the mixture of the gap. The materials of the unit TA-4 are: three fragments of wall of small size and reducing baking, and two fragments of wall of mixed baking and thin degreasing. One of them has its edges rolled, while the other shows a smoothed surface. A more attractive view is presented by the ceramics remains of the unit TA- 3. The following ones stand out among them (figure 2.2.A):

1. Three decorated fragments which form a very thin piece (figure 2.2.A.1), slighty rolled, concave in its longitudinal profile and convexe in the transverse one. It is characterized by the presence of two rounded rims or borders. One of them parallel to the longitudinal axis, and other that is normal to this. This one is slighty thickened. It is a ceramic piece made, apparently, on a thin plate that was probably leaned against an irregular surface (ground), since it shows a smoothed side, the decorated one, and other one quite irregular. Maybe, it was just the wish of finishing finely the decorated side, and for that, it was smoothed when the piece was already made and the paste was still soft. Its morphology appeals: the rim forms a 90° angle, which could be a fragment of handle. The degreasing is thick (> 2mm) and mainly, limy. The baking is oxidizing, its inside is reducing. The decoration consists of two lines of discontinuous incisive strokes in the thickened side of the edge, from them, five lines go at right angles: the two first, which come from the second rim, are formed again by discontinuous incisive strokes; secondly, there are three continuous incisive lines. The composition concludes with two lines of discontinuous incisive strokes; therefore, the decorative structure of the preserved fragment is completely symmetrical. If we consider that the undecorated ceramic fragment, the one that shows some of carbonated concretion, is a handle, then, we can think that the same decorative pattern could be repeated in the missing part.

2. This is a fragment that, as it happens with the previous piece, presents two orthogonal rims with a longitudinal profile, slightly concave and transversal convexe. It shows superficial carbonate concretions. It is hardly rolled (figure 2.2.A.2). It shows a main rim slightly thickened with a flat lip which turns suddenly, leaving an angle inferior to 90° in this case; and gets the same thickness than the rest of the piece. Now, the lip appears rounded. It presents a mixed baking with colouration changes, mainly among light greys and pale oranges. Both, the internal and external surfaces seem smoothed and the thickness changes reveal again slow rotations during its making. Here, the degreasing is also limy and it may include small vegetable fibres.

3. Fragment of wall of carenated ceramic. The inflection is appreciated both, in the internal and the external side of the piece (figure 2.2.A.3). It has been made with a slow rotation (handmade ceramic), where changes of thickness are very frequent in the same horizontal line. The baking is mixed. It is mainly oxidizing in the superior side of the careening and reducing in the inferior one. The paste is quite decanted and the degreasing is almost imperceptible at first sight. It presents limy concretions in the external side mainly. The edges are not rolled and it presents superficial carbonated concretions.

4. Rolled ceramic (fragment of wall) with an external inflection marked by a horizontal careen (figure 2.2.A.4). The baking and the degreasing are identical to those of the piece number 1, as well as the decoration, which is based on small strokes of burin. They form four parallel lines to the careen, and tend to horizontality together with the rests of to prints which are perpendicular to these. The external side, as it happens with the piece of number 1, has a more careful finish than the internal one, which has many irregularities. It belongs to the usual name of handmade ceramic, which can be named again as ceramics made with slow rotations. All this seems to indicate that this fragment and the one of the number 1 belonged to the same piece.

5. Four bottom fragments (see description 8) (figures 2.2.A.5, 2.2.A.6, 2.2.A.7 and 2.2.A.8): The base of the pieces is flat. The thickness of the bottom is out of proportion as regards the thickness of the start of the preserved wall. They seem to be made by slow rotation. Instead of using sticks/bars of paste, it seems that a very liquid paste has been applied using the fingers, and lately, it has been smoothed with the hands or with a spatula. There are areas in the external side where the smoothing is not homogeneous; therefore, layers of clay that were previously applied can be seen. The baking is mixed: the external side of the piece tends to be oxidizing while the internal side is reducing. There are several sizes of degreasing. It presents rests of soot in the external side, so that it can be inferred an use to cook food by putting the piece

directly beside the fireplace. One of the pieces (figure 2.2.A.7) has some very remarkable changes of thickness considering the small size of the preserved fragment. Its degreasing is limy, scanty but it has a big size (fragments of 3-4 mm). These four fragments present a bad condition. Two of them stand out because of its marked rolling

The differences in the baking do not show different moments, since, in this kind of batches made in mono-chamber ovens (holes in the ground where the pots are put and covered with firewood), the baking of each pot changes a lot according to the place they are inside the oven, and also, if the pieces are in close contact to the combustion. The degreasings, mainly limy, could show that the place where the earthenware was taken is quite near the settlement. Considering the described materials and their secondary position within the same level, this small ceramic collection does not allow us to do great chronocultural appraisals. However, two ceramic groups can be distinguished in a first approach. There is a first lot of several fragments which contains the two mentioned rims and the decorated fragments, which we associate to Neolithic. The second one is a small group that includes the carenated fragment, which could belong to a more advanced period, possibly to Copper Age.

Faunal remains

The malacological rests are scanty and come from subunit TA-3a and subunit TA-4. This group is only composed of gastropods. A specimen of *Palella (Patella) vulgata* (Linné, 1758), recuperated in TA-3a, stands out. The rest of the group belongs to three different kinds of continental gastropods that were found in the two mentioned units.

With regards to macromammals, the zooarchaeological analysis of the group shows the following spectrum of species: *Bos taurus*, *Ovis aries* or *Capra hircus* among the domesticated ones, and *Sus scropha*, *Orictolagus cuniculus*, *Cervus elaphus*, *Ursus arctos* and *Vulpes vulpes* among the wild ones. The lot of bones is composed of 203 rests; the ones of unit TA-3 stand out among them because they are the more numerous group (table 2.2). Compared to unit TA-3, unit TA-4 is no representative; it can be stood out the lack of animals of big size and the presence of rests of some kind of ovicaprid.

The bones of Torca l'Arroyu presents a very well preserved fauna. It has only turned out to be representative the fauna belonging to unit TA-3, since unit TA-4 contains few rests. The boar stands out among the documented animals; with regard to the domestic ones, the presence of the cow stands out. The presence of the ovicaprids is testimonial and little meaningful. The taphonomic and seasonal data allow to claim that the boars were hunted during summertime and the beginning of winter. In the case of the rest of the animals, the lack of seasonal data does not allow us to know when they died;

but the taphonomic information indicates, as it occurs with the boar, that the different animals of units TA-3 and TA-4 were processed by the human being, except for the fox, which lacks of cutting marks and its rests are not fragmented. Despite we can explain the represented fauna and its consequences to the human being, the existence of other alterations indicates that we face a group slanted by different processes. The presence of rolled and polished bones in unit TA-3 evidences that we are before a bone group moved by hydric transport. In the same way, the scavenger action of carnivores suggests that they acted on the bone sample slanting it. Therefore, we can think that these two agents could slant the bone sample and, at the same time, they can be also the main responsible ones of the high trampling that the bone rests show. The real importance of the fauna of Torca L'Arroyu is based on the presence of domestic fauna in a precise moment of the Asturian Neolithic and also, because of the predominance of the boar among the wild species.

GEOCHRONOLOGY: RADIOCARBONIC DATES

In order to obtain numeric ages for the site of Torca L'Arroyu, we sent five samples of charcoal and bone material coming from two different archaeological levels, TA-3 and TA-4 to the Laboratory of Radiocarbonic Date of the University of Barcelona, finally, they got reduced to four samples (figure 2.1.B).

Table 2.1 shows the source unit of the samples, the material, the code of laboratory, the date assignation results expressed in BP[1](1) with its uncertainty belonging to once the usual deviation of the radiometric measures that we indicate ordered from minor to major age. It also shows the results of the dates calibration according to CalPal 2005 SFCP curve (Weniger *et al.*, 2005). The probability intervals are indicated, whose sum is equal to 95,4% (calibration 2 sigma) (Stuiver y Reimer 1993), expressed in calendaric years cal. BP and cal. BC/AD[2].

TORCA L´ARROYU: NEOLITHIC SETTLEMENT, FIRES AND SEDIMENT PROCESSES

Considering the information exposed before, the first to be distinguished, on studying the sediment filling of Torca l'Arroyu, is that although it is a site located in a secondary position, it contains a very interesting geoarchaeologic information that we will try to decode

---

[1] BP (before present). It is used to indicate a radiocarbonic date expressed in its own chronological scale, which comes from the year 1950 dC. It is always presented through two values: the experimental value and the usual deviation belonging to the group of the radiometric measures. (Mestres, 2000a, 2000b).

[2] Cal BC (before Christ). It is used to indicate a date in the sun chronologic scale; it is expressed in years before Christ. It comes from the calibration of a radiocarbonic date.

Cal AD (annus Domini). It is used to indicate a calibrated date that comes from a radiocarbonic date. It is expressed in sun years after Christ.

Tab. 2.1. Torca L'Arroyu. Taxonomic profiles according to NR and MNI

Unit	TA-3		TA-4		Surface		MNI TA-3	MNI TA-4	MNI Surface
Taxon	NR	%	NR	%	NR	%	Ad/ Juv/ Inf	Ad/ Juv/ Inf	Ad/ Juv/ Inf
Bos taurus	22	12.3			2	22.2	1/1/0		1/0/0
Big	51	32.9			1	11.1			
Deer			1	4.5				1/0/0	
Average	2	1.3	1	4.5					
Boar	50	32.3					1/0/2	1/0/0	
Ovicaprid indet.	1		5	22.7				1/0/0	
Samall	22	14.2	11	50	4	44.4			
Bear	1	0.6					1/0/0		
Fox		0.0	4	18.2				1/0/0	
Rabbit					2	22.2			1/0/0
Indet.	24	6.5							
Total	173		22		9		3/1/2	4/0/0	2/0/0

NR: Number of remains; MNI: Minimal number of individuals; Ad.: Adult; Juv: Juvenile; Inf.: Infantile

Tab. 2.2. Torca L´Arroyu. Calibrated Radiocarbonic Dates

Unidat	Material	Code	^{14}C dates BP	2 σ calibrated dates cal. BP (0=AD1950)	2 σ calibrated dates cal. BC/AD
TA-4	Charcoals	UBAR-746	2050 ± 120	2340 – 1740 cal. BP	390 cal. BC – 210 cal. AD
TA-3b	Charcoals	UBAR-745	3190 ± 150	3790 – 3030 cal. BP	1840 – 1080 cal. BC
TA-3^a	Bones indet.	UBAR-804	4240 ± 60	4940 – 4580 cal. BP	2990 – 2630 cal. BC
TA-3^a	Bones of *Bos taurus*	UBAR-803	4930 ± 70	5850 – 5530 cal. BP	3900 – 3580 cal. BC

along this work. The hypothetical geodynamic model that we lay out considers the previous existence of an open air site located in the slope where the sinkhole opens. It is in a topographic position superior to the sinkhole. In this way, the slope and the small hill where the slope ends up offer excellent conditions for the habitat, with a South orientation and with a good sight control over the near fluvial bed of the Nora river. The chronology of this occupation of surface is marked by the date UBAR-803 4930 ± 70 BP (5850-5530 cal. BP), obtained from bone rests of an only specimen of *Bos taurus*. It locates the settlement in the first half of IV millenium a.c. (3900-3580 cal. BC) (figure 2.2.B). The length of this occupation would be defined by the date obtained from a sample that contains several bones, UBAR-804 4240 ± 60 BP (4940- 4580 cal. BP) (figure 2.2.B), so that its result would be the mean of its different ages; it would show us an average chronology for the settlement, which would go along the first third of the III milenium B.C. (2990-2630 cal. BC). If we sum the probabilities of both dates, the period of validity for the settlement would be in the interval 5860-4610 cal. BP (3910-2660 cal. BC), whose considered duration is 1250 years. This long duration of the inhabitation of the slope settlement together with the

presence of ceramic materials that seem to belong to two different moments would be showing us the existence of two moments of inhabitation: one of them would belong to the Neolithic, associated to the date UBAR-803, which the decorated ceramics would come from, and the other one, to the Copper Age, associated to the date UBAR-804, the carenated ceramics belong to it. The first moment would be related to the Neolithic levels of some other Asturian sites such as the A2 level of the Cave of Mazaculos (González Morales, 1995) whose date is GAK-15221 5050 ± 120 BP (6040-5560 cal. BC) or the tumulus MAXII of Monte Areo (de Blas, 1999) whose date is CSIC-1380 5133 ± 30 BP (6000-5720 cal. BP; 4050-3770 cal. BC) (figure 2.2.B).

Inside the cavity, the sequence begins with some materials which are produced by the rock alteration of the substratum (unit TA-1). They fill in the existing paleotopography in the cavity ground and probably, were placed in a time when the cavity was without outside communication. The sequence continues when the conection of the cavity with the outside is made through a small collapse sinkhole which contains external materials.

After leaving the settlement of the slope, some of its rests and the thin geologic materials from the surface went through processes linked to a dynamic of gravity-slope with hydric influence due to rainfalls of some intensity. This produced clay layers, which are the source of unit TA-2.

Later, there was a fire in the slope and the vegetation was wiped out. As a consequence, the archaeological rests that were still there and the surface geological materials (thin and thick) went through a new sediment cycle by processes of gravity-slope with hydric influence, which are the source of the clay layers with pebbles and blocks that ended up in subunit TA-3a, whose inside contains a lot of archaeological materials (bone and ceramic rests, polished tools) and clear signs of hydric transport. The presence of big angular blocks of authoctonous lime in the base of TA-3a evidences that in those moments, there were collapses in the opening of the *torca*, which enlarged its original size. The sediment process of gravity-slope continues with the clay layer of subunit TA-3b dated in the interval 3790-3030 cal. BP (1840-1080 cal. BC), which has scanty lateral extension in the sediment cone, and with the clay layer with stones and blocks of subunit TA-3c, which superimposes on subunit TA-3a towards the distal areas of the cone. Both, TA-3b and TA-3c contain scattered and scanty archaeological rests, which evidences that the rests of the settlement of the slope surface were practically dismantled.

Later, the slope where the settlement was located went through another fire which wiped out its vegetal cover; besides, new episodes of dragging by gravity-slope processes took place and led to the sediment process of unit TA-4 dated in the interval 2340-1740 cal. BP (390 cal. BC-210 cal. AD), where two levels of well stratified ashes and charcoals can be seen in the clay sediments.

Finally, during a wet epoch with mild temperatures of some duration, the precipitation of the calcic carbonate took place. It formed the espeleotheme which sealed the deposits of the sinkhole. The precipitation continued over it, and stalagmites and stalactites were produced; in some cases they have formed small columns.

Bibliography

BARNOLAS, A.; PUJALTE, V. (eds.) (2004) La Cordillera Pirenaica. In: VERA, J.A. ed., *Geología de España*. Madrid: Sociedad Geológica de España – Instituto Geológico y Minero de España, p. 231-343.

BLAS CORTINA, M.A. (1999) Nuevas formas tumulares neolíticas en el Monte Areo. Excavaciones de 1995 a 1997. *Excavaciones Arqueológicas en Asturias 1995-1998*. Oviedo: Principado de Asturias. p. 101-110.

EIROA, J.J.; BACHILLER GIL, J.A.; CASTRO PÉREZ, L.; LOMBA MAURANDI, J. (1999) *Nociones de tecnología y tipología en Prehistoria*. Barcelona: Editorial Ariel S.A. 393 p.

FARIAS, P.; MARQUÍNEZ, J. (1995) El relieve. In: ARAMBURU, C.; BASTIDA, F., eds., *Geología de Asturias*. Gijón: Ediciones Trea. p.163-172.

GONZÁLEZ MORALES, M.R. (1995) Memoria de los trabajos de limpieza y toma de muestras en los yacimientos de las cuevas de Mazaculos y el Espinoso (La Franca, Ribadedeva) y la Llana (Andrín, Llanes) en 1993. *Excavaciones Arqueológicas en Asturias 1991-1994*. Oviedo: Principado de Asturias. p. 65-78.

MAPA GEOLÓGICO DE ESPAÑA E. 1:50.000, n° 29 (13-4) Oviedo. Madrid: Instituto Geológico y Minero de España, 1973.

MARTÍN-SERRANO, A. (1994) Macizo Hespérico Septentrional. In GUTIÉRREZ ELORZA, M., ed., *Geomorfología de España*. Madrid: Editorial Rueda, p. 25-62.

MARTÍNEZ GARCÍA, E. (1981) La geología y el relieve de Asturias. *Enciclopedia Temática de Asturias*. Gijón: Silverio Cañada, Ed., t.10, p. 57-124.

STUIVER, M.; REIMER, P. (1993) Extended Data Base and Revised CALIB 3.0 [14]C Age Calibration Program. *Radiocarbon*, 19 (1), p. 215-230.

STUIVER, M. [*et al*] (1998) INTCAL98 Radiocarbon Age Calibration 24,000-0 cal. BP. *Radiocarbon*, 40 (3), p.1041-1084.

WENINGER, B.; JÖRIS, O.; DANZEGLOCKE, U. (2005) *Glacial radiocarbon age conversion. Cologne radiocarbon calibration and palaeoclimate research package <CALPAL> User manual*. Köln: Universität zu Köln, Institut für Ur- und Frühgeschichte, Rdiocarbon Laboratory, 29 p.

FROM "INLAND NEOLITHIC" TO "NEOLITHIC DWELLING IN THE INLAND": THE ROLE OF HOMOGENEOUS AND HETEROGENEOUS ELEMENTS ON THE EXPLANATION OF EARLIER AGRICULTURAL STAGES IN CENTRAL SPAIN

Enrique CERRILLO CUENCA

Instituto de Arqueología – Mérida. Plaza de España, 15. 06800 Mérida (Badajoz). Spain.
E-mail: ecerrillo@iam.csic.es

Abstract: In early eighties, some Spanish archaeologists started to use the concept "inland Neolithic" to make reference to those rare sites with impressed vessels located in the inland areas of Iberia. This expression has been regularly used by those archaeologists who needed to name the archaeological findings as a new reality which differs from Neolithic coastal groups.

But in fact, the notion of "inland Neolithic" can be found in some writings of 1930's and 1940's by Bosch Gimpera and San Valero, who had proposed other concepts such as "Caves with decorated potteries Culture" and "Neolithic of the Plateau" to name it. Since that moment, the neolithic sites of several provinces of Spain and Portugal were supposed to be more recent than the caves sited near the shorelines of Spanish Levant and Andalusia, introducing an axiom that would no be easily forgotten.

Nowadays, some projects developed in inland Iberia have shown an intense Neolithic dwelling alongside the basin of Duero, Tagus and Guadiana rivers, in the spaces considered as being part of the former "Inland Neolithic".

Maybe, the "Inland Neolithic" concept was defined within a theoretical framework dominated by the lack of archaeological data, but, at the present time, its validity can be questioned by the large number of existing sites. In this paper I wish to discuss some concepts involved in the use of this expression rather than make a synthesis about the recent research in those territories. I think that many related concepts must be reviewed; especially those linked to the homogeneity of some cultural aspects and even what can and what can not be considered as "inland".

The homogeneous/inhomogeneous nature of Neolithic groups from the inland is analyzed in order to understand the process of neolithization: whether or not the origin of Neolithic in the Inland is the same in all territories (i.e. as result of a wide colonization), and even it is a useful way to "measure" the implication of "indigenous" components on the formation of agricultural landscapes.

Summing-up, I believe that is time to look for specific regional studies and understand the diversity of geographical environments in order to appreciate the emergence of agricultural practices in inland Iberia.

Key-Words: Iberia Inland Neolithic; Neolithization process; Agricultural landscapes

Resumo: No início da década de 80, alguns arqueólogos espanhóis utilizaram o conceito "Neolítico Interior" para classificar alguns, raros, sítios com cerâmicas impressas, localizados no interior do espaço peninsular, e que se diferenciavam dos grupos neolíticos conhecidos nas regiões costeiras.

No entanto, o conceito "Neolítico Interior" pode ser já encontrado na bibliografia produzida, nas décadas de 30 e 40, por Bosch Gimpera e San Valero, que propuseram os termos "Cultura de grutas com cerâmicas decoradas" e "Neolítico da Meseta" para designar essas realidades. Desde então, considerou-se que os sítios neolíticos de diferentes regiões de Espanha e Portugal, seriam mais recentes que a ocupação das grutas localizadas no litoral levantino e na Andaluzia, introduzindo no debate um axioma de difícil contestação.

Neste momento, alguns projectos a decorrer no interior da Península Ibérica, demonstraram a existência de uma intensa ocupação neolítica ao longo das bacias do Douro, do Tejo e do Guadiana, portanto nas áreas tradicionalmente integradas no "Neolítico Interior".

Este conceito construído num quadro teórico marcado pela escassez de informação arqueológica pode, hoje, ser discutido em função do importante número de sítios já detectados. Neste trabalho, discutem-se alguns conceitos associados a esta designação que necessitam de urgente revisão, designadamente os que admitem a homogeneidade de alguns aspectos culturais e os que rodeiam os conceitos de "interior."

A homogeneidade/heterogeneidade dos grupos neolíticos do Interior é analisada tendo em vista o processo de neolitização; a origem comum, ou distinta, deste Neolítico do Interior (em consequência de um processo de colonização); a participação e o contributo das realidades indígenas na formação das paisagens agrícolas.

Em suma, este parece o momento para desenvolver análises regionais e analisar o papel da diversidade de ambientes geográficos no quadro da emergência das práticas agrícolas no interior peninsular.

Palavras-chave: Neolítico Interior; Processo de Neolitização; Paisagens Agrícolas

In 1980, M.D. Fernández-Posse published her work about the excavations of El Aire's cave at Patones (Madrid). She stated that many of decorated sherds, manly with impressed and incised motives, could be related to some cultural context from Andalusia, where the research on Neolithic had a strong tradition on the study of pottery. In fact, this archaeologist proposed that some sites with impressed pottery in Central Spain would be related to a same cultural group defined apparently by its poor archaeological documentation (Fernández-Posse 1980). She used the "inland Neolithic" expression to make reference to those dispersal sites in Northern and Southern Plateau which shared the common attribute of impressed vessels. In that moment, a new cultural concept

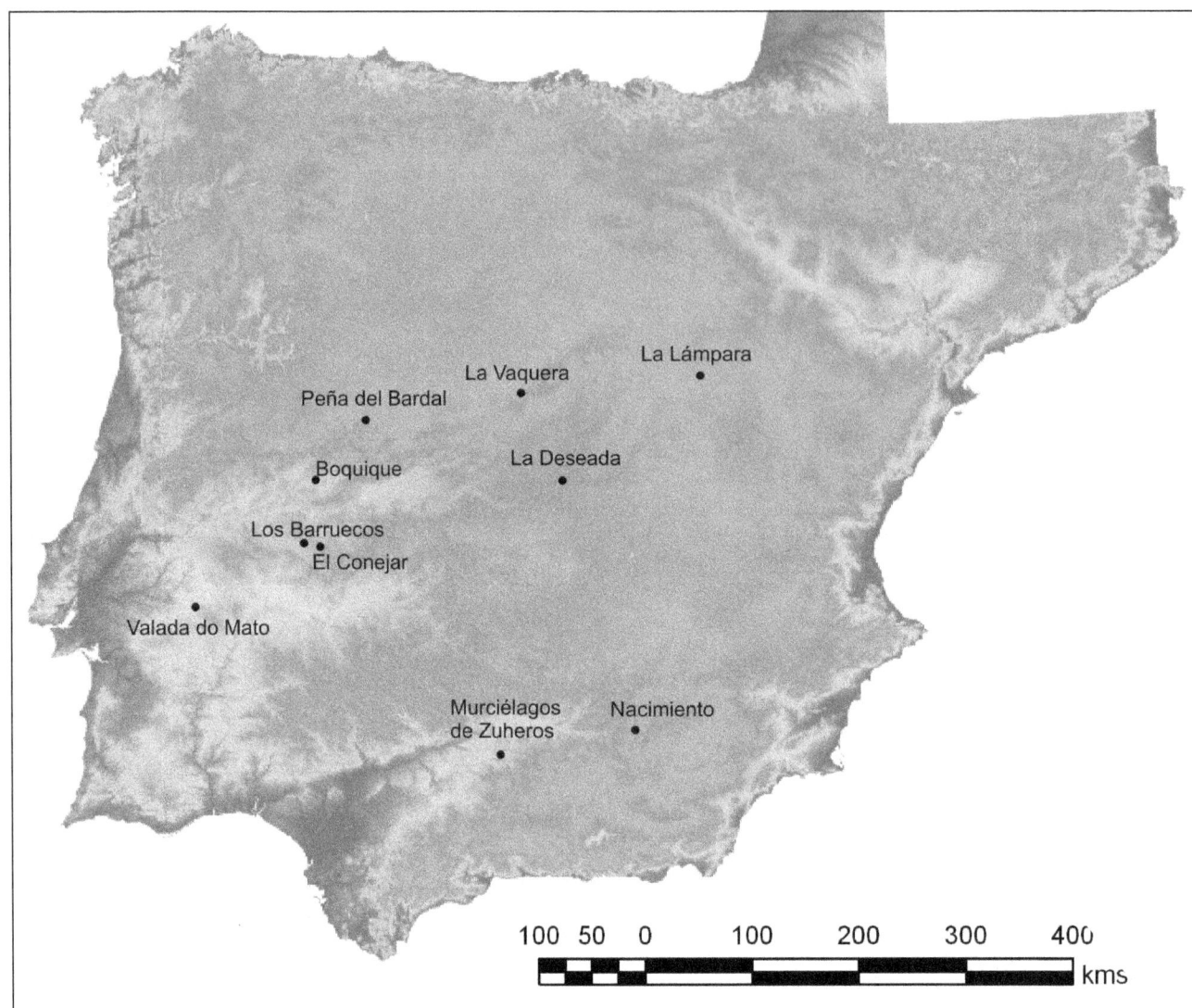

Fig. 3.1. Location of some Early Neolithic sites cited in text

was born, and it would have a frequent presence in Spanish archaeological literature during the eighties and nineties decades.

Nevertheless "Inland Neolithic" is not really an original concept by itself, some ideas can be found in early writings about the Iberian Neolithic. Since the 1930's and 1940's decade Bosch Gimpera (1945) and San Valero (1946) had been working in the cultural delimitation of Iberian Neolithic groups on the territory. P. Bosch Gimpera (1945) distinguished four groups in Neolithic Iberia. Among them, the "Central Culture" or "Caves with Decorated Pottery Culture" is the one that involves a significant part of inner Iberia. J. San Valero (1946) stated that there were five Neolithic groups in Iberia; among them, the "Plateau (Meseta) Neolithic" can be understood as a primary definition of "Inland Neolithic".

The study of "Inland Neolithic" and its cultural systemization was the aim of two brief works published by Antona (1986) and Municio (1988) in the eighties, both authors gather data from inner Neolithic sites and try to explain the human presence in Central Iberia during Neolithic. The same expression has been used by Portuguese scholars to refer the sites located far from the Atlantic shore, in the inner lands of Portugal. Despite the historiographical origin of this expression is neatly different from Spain, the same procedure seems to be implied in its use. In fact, the archaeological knowledge and documentation of Neolithic realities in inner lands of Tagus, Douro and Guadiana basins is clearly posterior to the first data about Early Neolithic at diverse lands.

In both cases, there is an underlying question that has been reinforced by later interpretations of the neolithization process: the spread of agriculture and livestock breeding towards inner lands of Iberia would be produced as the result of a demic colonization of unhabited territories. Several Spanish (Kunst & Rojo 1999) or Portuguese (Zilhão 2003) archaeologist have supported this hypothesis taking into account the lack of Mesolithic records in Central Spain, and even the existing delay among Early Neolithic of Spanish Levant and inner territories. In fact, the chronological criteria used are extremely based on cross-cultural comparison of pottery traditions, one of them has often been the presence of absence of cardial wares types (Juan-Cabanilles & Martí 2002: 61-62). Thus, following up this cultural interprettation, Neolithic sites with cardial wares could be doubtless interpreted as Early Neolithic sites and those sites with no evidence of cardial really correspond to advanced stages of neolitization process. This "late" tradition has different names. In Portugal, after Guilaine and Ferreira paper (1970) the called "Furinha horizon" would represent the stage of substitution of cardial ware by local styles. That period was formerly called "Early Evolved Neolithic" in Portugal, or just "Epicardial" in Spain.

During the late nineties the growth of fieldwork has carried out just in Portugal or in Spain, many researchers have oriented their projects to accomplish the study of early agricultural stages in different territories of Inland Iberia. The research was primarily focused to obtain cultural indicators of Neolithic presence in the interior lands of Iberia. The University of Valladolid has developed three interesting projects in Northern Plateau, at the sites of La Velilla (Delibes & Zapatero 1996), La Vaquera (Estremera 2003) or La Lámpara (Kunst & Rojo 2000), even from South Plateau new data are being included, among several works: Bueno et al. (1995), Rubio & Blasco (2005), Villa & Rojas (1996) or Jiménez (2005). Other inner regions as Alentejo (Diniz 2003) or Spanish Extremadura (Cerrillo 2005) are incorporating new data in recent times to the analysis of this period. The results have shown some interesting facts that are contradictory to cultural interpretations about the delay on the arrival of agriculture and even the presence of late hunter-gathers in those territories.

This paper tries to reflect on some concepts brought out by the acquisition of new data, but manly my intention is to gather some facts which show that there are some common elements on Early Neolithic groups from Inland Iberia and, what is more important, regional character-ristics that show how difficult is to explain the whole process from an unidirectional approach. As far as the published works are starting to show, there are hetero-geneous components among Neolithic groups of Inland Iberia, we are not also speaking in terms of material culture, but about several significant differences on landscapes and its formation.

During the last years, my research has focused on one of these regions from Inland Iberia: the river Tagus basin (Cerrillo 2005) on the current region of Spanish Extrema-dura. The basin of Tagus is a territory where the archa-eological experience lets us to think about a more com-plex process of neolithization in which we must take into account new factors. Along this text, I will frequently use this space as a paradigm of those inner lands, not just by the obtained results, but also because the fieldwork deve-loped can be used to make comparisons to closer areas.

What are the true borders of Inland Neolithic is a question to be specified. The present geopolitical organization of inner Iberia actually distorts an optimal appreciation of the diversity of neolithic groups. In a recent paper (Arias et al. in press) we intended to make a primary distribution of inner and coastal areas by the means of a GIS cartographical model which take into account the orographical characteristics of terrain and distances in order to estimate the accessibility from the coast of some territories. The more evident result is that some sites considered so far as belonging to different groups of Iberian Neolithic are located as interiorly as some others considered as coastal group (i.e. Andalusian groups). In fact, some well known sites such as Murciélagos de Zuheros (Gavilán et al. 1996) or Nacimiento de Pontones (Asquerino y López 1981) considered as belonging to Andalusian Neolithic groups are as located as far from coast as some Plateau sites. This fact shows the nullity of linear processes described for the whole peninsula and the need to consider a geographical shade in order to achieve a better comprehension of the process.

In 1980's, the "Inner Neolithic" concept was applied to explain as a whole reality some sites with apparent common pottery styles, often without stratigraphical or chronological information (i.e. data from survey or not contextualized sherds). Thus, by the means of it, the available evidence of theoretically unhabited territories were grouped stressing some cultural affinities such as the absence of cardial pottery. After more than twenty years, several projects have shown the diversity of material culture, landscapes and the antiquity of first crops in Iberia. By the regional observation of cultural processes we can state that there is a dialectic between own and shared issues (i.e. pottery styles and frequencies) among several Iberian geographies. Nevertheless, in practice, "Inner Neolithic" is rather a more geographical than cultural concept. By the means of it, all the scarce archaeological evidence was grouped in a wide space with a lack of dwelling to offer a more satisfactory explanation of neolithization. So "Inland Neolithic" concept has indeed developed a historiographical dimension which cannot be misunderstood when used.

Several authors have pleaded for a colonization process of Inner Iberia, taking into account the lack of Mesolithic data (Zilhão 2003: 213-214), or even the inexistence of cardial wares (Juan-Cabanilles & Martí 2000: 64), both arguments will lead to see demic diffusion as a serious alternative to explain first Neolithic crops. As I have exposed (Cerrillo 2005: 31), one of the main question is if Neolithic groups from Inner Iberia have common characteristics which let us talk about heterogeneous components on its formation, and what could be more interesting, formal cultural differences on its early context of formation.

Nevertheless, the question of a common origin is still open and depends on the real presence of dwelling before the agricultural practices would have consolidated.

During the last years our research in Spanish Extremadura has clearly revealed the presence of at least two shelters with artifacts and AMS dating which clearly shows that inner basin of Tagus river was occupied during the VIIIth millenium cal BC. At El Conejar cave (Cerrillo Cuenca 1999), the team of Prof. Carbonell has obtained the date of 8220+/-40 BP (7355-7078 cal BC[1]) from a small breccia with quartzite macrolithic tools and faunal remains (Canals *et al.* 2005: 65). This cave was lately occupied by neolithic and chalcolithic communities as some artifacts can prove. Our recent works in Canaleja Gorge have indeed supplied some data about Mesolithic and Early Neolithic dwelling in shelters located at the bottom of valley. At Canaleja 2 shelter we found a few evidence of geometrics and microlaminar tools associated to a hearth, whose charcoals have been dated in 8740+/-40 BP (Beta-214600; 7940-7611 cal BC). The same shelter would be occupied later during Early Neolithic as some sherds of "boquique"[2] ware show.

By inserting this absolute dates within a wider framework, we find a real correspondence with panels from a new rock-art cycle which has been recently documented in several locations of Spanish Extremadura (Collado 2005). Despite we found the most important proof of contemporaneous occupations on Portugal, where Prazo (Rodrigues & Angelucci 2004) and Barca de Xarez Baixo (Almeida *et al.* 1999) sites with similar absolute dates from VIIIth cal BC. Going further the documentation of Mesolithic sites in Inland Iberia is significantly increasing (Arias *et al.* in press), i.e. innerest areas as Madrid are providing in recent times information about last hunter-gathers (Morín de Pablos *et al.* 2006). Nevertheless, according to these dates, we must stress that at least in Spanish Extremadura there is still an important gap between the dated Mesolithic occupations and the earlier agricultural context, which are situated around the 5500 cal BC.

Within the current archaeological record of Mesolithic sites is really hard to determine what the degree of homogeneity in landscape or in material culture is. As far as we can see we could defend that there are at least two different tendencies in material culture, one defined by the use of local raw material as quartz or quartzite (i.e. Barca do Xarez, El Conejar) and probably some sites where the use of flint becomes more obvious. Despite the chronological gap between Mesolithic and Early Neolithic, if we put together different data from inner Iberia we can observe that is possible to plead for continuity. Thus, there is still some inability to contrast new models, a situation than can undergo changes with the achievement of new dates. There has been a fairly neat progression on the publication of dates. Duiring the late eighties only TL dates from La Vaquera cave were published (Rubio & Blasco 1988-89), on the contrary,

nowadays absolute dates for inner Neolithic dwelling are considerably increasing. From La Vaquera comes a range of dates from VIth to IVth millennia (Estremera 2003) comprising all the neolithic phases. Three dates from the basal leveles of this cave are significantly ancient (GrN-22931, 7050±70 BP, 6052-5775 cal BC; GrN-18340, 6780±180 BP; 6021-5376 cal BC and GrN-17386, 6760±80 BP, 5835-5527 cal BC) but the author denies its validity considering that: a) are too ancient in comparison with other dates from the same phase, b) there are no dates as ancient as these ones in Inland Iberia, and c) the recovered material culture does not match with the provided temporal gap. I would no consider these reasons as determinant, because an aditional explanation of such chronological gap, defined by three different dates, should be given. In addition, M. Rojo Guerra *et al.* (in this volume) has presented similar and even more ancient dates coming from different contexts of La Vaquera site and expanding the problem further than a concrete site or statrigraphical question. Following the publication of a previous paper (Kunst & Rojo 2000), La Vaquera chronological gap was established *circa* the middle of VIth millennium cal BC. Unavoidably, we must consider a proper explanation for this set of ancient dates. The first possibility is that the dates that comes from the fringe after 6700 BP are really contemporaneous to earliest peasant dwelling of Atlantic and Mediterranean shore-lines, such as Caldeirão (Zilhão 1992), Buraca Grande (Zilhão 2000) or Margineda (Guilaine *et al.* 1995). It would be more difficult to give explanation to more ancient dates, which could hypotetically disguise Meso-lithic occupations.

One of the hot spot is the analysis of neolithic landscapes, which can determine the convergence of common factors on the formation of agricultural groups. In the case of Spanish Extremadura the similarities with the documented patterns of settlement in Alentejo are evident (Calado 2000). In both areas there is a preferential occupation of granite areas and more rarely limestone shelters, this fact shows a peculiar adaptation to landscape which differs from other territorial areas from inner Iberia.

Following the few AMS available dates we can propose that this agricultural adaptation would be carried out during the second half of VIth millenium, despite the range of dates is not enough wide and it would be necessary to obtain more data in certain enclosed areas. In any case, we could also support a variability of dwelling in a regional scale. In Spanish Extremadura we could defend a non-specialised system of production which looks up for the use of several natural resources. Moreover, in the case of karstic systems there is a clear coincidence among the territories of hunter-gather groups during the VIIIth millennium and subsequent neolithic landscapes.

In any case, we start to document a variety on the use of natural resources and the variety of crops. In a recent paper, L. Zapata *et alii* (2003) state the variety of crops

---

[1] All dates have been calibrated to 2 sigma using OxCal 4.0 software and IntCal 0'4 curve.

[2] "Boquique" ware is actually a kind of impressed pottery well known in early stages of Iberian Neolithic.

Tab. 3.1. Some evidence of agriculture and livestock breeding on Tagus inner basin

Site	Direct evidence	Dates	Geology
Barruecos	Cereal Pollen, and Cereal phytoliths	6080+/-40 BP	Granite
Barruecos	Bone of sheep?	6060+/-50 BP	Granite
C. Horca	Cereal Pollen	Not dated	Granite
Canaleja II	Cereal Pollen	Not dated	Limestone
Conejar	Seeds (mainly free-threshing wheats)	Neolithic?	Limestone

Tab. 3.2. Early Neolithic storage pits in inner Iberia

Site	Region	Evidence	Absolute dates (only from pits)	References
Valada do Mato	Alentejo(Portugal)	Pit (UE 18)	not available	Diniz 2003
La Deseada	Madrid (Spain)	Pits (4000, 8100 and 3700)	not available	Díaz del Río & Consuegra 1999
La Lámpara	Soria (Spain)	Pits	6421±30 BP	Rojo & Kunst 2000
Mesegar de Tajo	Toledo (Spain)	Pits (IV y XVI)	not available	Villa & Rojas 1996
Los Barruecos	Extremadura (Spain)	Covered pits (UE 117 y 134)	6080±40 BP 6060±50 BP	Cerrillo Cuenca 2005

documented in the earliest neolithic sites of inner Iberia such as La Lámpara or La Vaquera and particularly, taking into account the lack of free-threshing wheat, so common in other Iberian neolithic sites. As the authors appoint, the scarce volume of data in this wide area only allows to make suppositions, so the hypothesis of agricultural adaptations of crops to diverse geographical backgrounds or a mere cultural variety product are still to be determined. We must add that these biological data could be related with material culture to try to determine the cultural homogeneity of earlier agricultural groups.

In West Center Iberia, the neolithic production raises new questions about the development of agriculture. Firstly, we must consider an early interaction with forest. As pallynological analyses from Los Barruecos testify, Neolithic communities would develop a non-intensified land use (López Sáez et al. 2005), and even we can track some gathering activities of acorn. The recovery of biological evidence of crops and faunal remains in sites dominated by acid soils, whose geology is often formed by granite decomposition, is an almost impossible task. The documentation of agricultural evidences at the sites of Extremadura (table 3.1) shows anyway this fact and the need to turn to other types of analysis to get a proof for cropping activities. Pallynological identification (López Sáez et al. 2005) of cereal has become the more efficient way to fix a true cerealistic production, whose repercussion on the environment is evident. Even phytoliths analyses, not commonly used to register evidences of production, shows the consumption of barley (Juan-Tresserras & Matamala 2006). The recovery of seeds only

could be carried out at El Conejar cave (Canals et al. 2005), where naked wheat and escanda could suggest well established neolithic croppings, nevertheless the absence of stratigraphy for Holocene occupations must be considered when establishing a date for them.

Actually, there are several Early Neolithic sites where we can prove the existence of pit-storage structures which can be interpreted as silos in adjacent spaces to habitat. Some pits have been documented alongside Tagus basin, from Madrid to Lisboa, taking into account the results of excavations from La Deseada (Díaz del Río & Consuegra 1999), Mesegar de Tajo (Villa & Rojas 1996), Los Barruecos (Cerrillo Cuenca et al. 2006) and São Pedro de Canaferrim (Simões 2003). Other sites from Douro and Guadiana basins reflect the same predisposition, silos have been found at La Lámpara (Rojo & Kunst 2000) or Valada do Mato (Diniz 2003). The data from these sites with silos reflects the common need for surplus storage, and the verification of low-intensity cultivation on their environment. Relative and absolute chronologies points out the late of VIth millennium or the transit from VIth to V[th] as the beginning of these sites, as shown in table 3.2. So the absolute dates from some of these structure and storage vessels seem to be a good element to reinforce the agricultural vocation of these sites.

Pottery and its decoration styles have often lead the cultural indicators of neolitization process, despite nowadays its value has been in decline with more frequent publications of well-defined contexts from the point of view of subsistencial data and absolute dates,

Tab. 3.3. Elements to analyse intra-regional variability in Spanish Extremadura

Kind of settlement	Sites	Evidence of crops	Pottery	Lithics	Geological Background	Occupations
Shelthers in slopes	Boquique Atambores Peña Aguilera	Hand mills (indirect)	Predominance of open vessels	Scarce microlaminar, geometrics	Always granite	Discontinuity Late Bronze Age (Boquique)
On hillocks	Barruecos C. de la Horca Cerca Antonio Mingo Martín	Cereal pollen Phytoliths Storage pits Hand mills	Predominance of open vessels, presence of storage vessels	Scarce microlaminars, few geometrics	Often granite, very rare on schist	Discontinuity Middle Neolithic dated Chalcolithic dated
Close to rivers	Cañadilla C. los Lobos Valdecañas	Hand mills (indirect)	(absence of diggings)	Scarce microlaminars, geometrics	Always granite (also possible on schist)	Only Neolithic (apparently, no diggings seasons)
Caves	Conejar Canaleja I Canaleja II	Seeds Cereal pollen	Predominance of open vessels	Scarce microlaminars, geometrics	Limestone	Discontinuity Mesolithic dated Middle Neolithic others

Tab. 3.4. Critical aspects on determining the degree of innovation from some elements of Early Neolithic dwelling

Element	Nature	Critical aspect
Mesolithic dwelling	Heterogeneity?	The is a lack of data from VIIth and VIth millennia
Landscape	Heterogeneity	Intra-regional analyses should be strengthened
Production	Heterog. / Homog.	More data from cropping is needed
Material culture analyses	Heterogeneity	Some homogeneous elements (in pottery), lithics
Chronologies	Homogeneity	The process appears to be contemporaneous in inland Iberia, but several dates would improve models

nevertheless it became soon a strong argument to make comparision between geographical areas. The vectors of demic diffusion proposed during 1980's and 1990's make no sense today, when we now that settlements can be understood as participative places that receive material and cultural influences from far regions. For example, some decorative patterns, as boquique pottery, have an excellent representation on inner sites, meanwhile others have an uneven presence. In the last years some cardial wares have been identified in central areas of Iberia, despite some sherds need to be re-analyzed. For instance some cardial decorated sherds come from Northern Plateau, one from the megalithic collective burial of El Torrejón de Villamayor (Arias & Jiménez 1994: 15), whose presence have not been explained yet in a satisfactory way. A collection of cardial ware sherds were recuperated at the site of Peña del Bardal (Gutiérrez 1966) in 1950's among others neatly Neolithic pottery remains. Recently, the excavations of Verona II site in Madrid province seem to have supplied some dubious sherds with cardial decoration (Jiménez 2005: 908). We must stress (Cerrillo 2005: 95) that some impressed sherds have decorations similar to cardial, just repeating the same patterns where the imprinting of shell cannot be determined easily. That is the case of some sherds from Mesegar de Tajo (Villa & Rojas 1996) or even some

fragments from El Conejar and Boquique caves. Somehow, the old perception of the relationship between shorelines and inner environments is still valid, despite it must be more delimited and clarified. Taking into account the dialectical discourse used in this paper, we can admit that the presence of some cardial wares in inner lands do not have influence on the individual development of different territories, regardless of this archaeographical element possesses tinges of homogeneity.

We still do not have percentages of pottery characteristics for several inner sites from Iberia, which would help to define theoretical geographic areas further on the absence/presence of concrete attributes. A proof of these variations between the inner areas themselves is shown by choosing different terms of comparison, i.e. the sites from Tagus basin and La Vaquera cave. For instance comparing the percentage of decorated pottery, we find real differences. There we can state some territorial differences among joins of material culture that contrast with the vector transmission proposed for productive practices following the dispersion of certain pottery styles. Thus, the values of two uneven shared elements like red varnish and Boquique pottery question these "paths" of novelties diffusion and, moreover, shows different tendencies on the called "Inner Neolithic". It is not possible to follow vectors of diffusion as thought some decades ago; i.e. "red varnish pottery" is present in west Andalusia and Meseta, but is really scanty in Extremadura. Thus, the similarities in pottery joins from areas could show different territorial behaviour that could be tracked as hypothesis in a pre-neolithic tradition[3]. At least, in pottery joins there are not clear homogeneous elements in Central Iberia, except by the practical lack of cardial pottery, which cannot actually be used as a common sign of entropy.

If not related to evidences of production and absolute dates, pottery should not be used as an element to explain by itself the neolithization process. Thus, the theoretical "epicardial ware" horizon should be questioned when trying to explain the neolithization process as a regional derivation from cardial ware (Alday 2006: 640). In fact, some cardial sherds show clear relationships with coastal areas but is not a determinant element which can be used to propose different cultural trends. However absolute dates and decoration shows that the earlier peasants in inner Iberia are contemporaneous to coastal cardial-wares groups, defining a more complex situation than in 1980's o 1990's. Fortunately, at the present times, the excavation of sites as Los Murciélagos (Gavilán *et al.* 1996), La Lámpara (Kunst & Rojo 2000) o La Vaquera (Estremera 2003) are providing enough data to understand the whole process from a more complete perspective. Therefore, absolute dates from each area are really the indicators that fix joins of pottery styles and specific agricultural strategies.

In inland Iberia there are territories that can be described by owning several peculiarities and developing production at the same period. If we think locally, we found that there is a high degree of intra-regional variability. As lack of documentation in areas with scarce data would be solved, we will have more terms of comparison that let us to state rigorously more specific models to study the transition to agriculture. The models based on the colonization of inlands usually defend the absence of settlement in inner Iberia during the beginnings of Holocene, a commonplace when trying to explain the "Inner Neolithic. With the historiographical overcome of that model is obvious that certain features does not points towards a unidirectional human colonization of Iberia inlands. Such process would produce a more homogeneous archaeographical image, as is evident in Central Europe with LBK groups. On the contrary, several differences on the types of habitat might reveal a previous tradition on the exploration of landscapes as Bugocki has pointed out (Bugocki 2003: 263). In inner Iberia the main problem is the real lack of surveys for most of the territory, and in some cases the

implication of recent anthropical distortion on landscapes (Cerrillo Cuenca 2005: 119), but as I set previously, we find some significant variations on intra-regional and regional levels. For instance, the use of caves and open-air settlements in diverse geological background shows a considerable degree of variation, but as far as the archaeological record can provide there are not differences among the economical activities, and even La Lámpara and La Vaquera sites can be equally compared (Rojo & Estremera 2000).

The varieties in landscapes could be used to describe a complex process. Thus, we can understand heterogeneity as cause of "interaction" and the role that previous dwelling played in the acquisition of cropping and stock-breeding. Heterogeneous components in material culture and biological remains of crops draw diverse models of interaction in parallel times. As far as the archaeological record becomes more explicit, we could find more indicators that will probably point to processes that are actually more complex.

References

ALDAY, A. 2006: El Neolítico Antiguo de Mendandia y la Radiocronología de la primitiva industria alfarera peninsular. In Alday, A.: *El legado arqueológico de los últimos cazadores en la Prehistoria de Treviño.* Memoria, Arqueología en Castilla y León 15: 639-668.

ALMEIDA, F., MAURICIO, J., SOUTO, P. & VALENTE, M.J. 1999: Novas perspectivas para o estudo do Epipaleolítico do interior alentejano: noticia preliminar sobre a descoberta do sítio arqueológico da Barca do Xarez Baixo, *Revista portuguesa de Arqueología* vol. 2, n. 1: 25-38.

ANTONA del VAL, V. 1986: Aproximación a la problemática del Neolítico en la Meseta: una propuesta de secuencia cultural, *Wad-Al-Hayara* 13: 9-45.

ARIAS CABAL, P., CERRILLO CUENCA, E., ÁLVAREZ, E., GÓMEZ-PELLÓN, E. & GONZÁLEZ CORDERO, A. In press: A view from the edges: the mesolithic settlement of the interior areas of the iberian peninsula reconsidered, *MESO 2006.* Belfast.

ARIAS GONZÁLEZ, L. & JIMÉNEZ GONZÁLEZ, M. C. 1994: Ídolo-placa y otras piezas funerarias procedentes del dolmen de "El Torrejón" (Villamayor-Salamanca), *Xábiga* 7: 8-17.

ASQUERINO, M. D. & LÓPEZ, P. 1981: La cueva del Nacimiento (Pontones). Un yacimiento neolítico en la Sierra del Segura, *Trabajos de Prehistoria* 38: 107-138.

BOSCH GIMPERA, P. 1945: *El poblamiento antiguo y la formación de los pueblos de España.* Mexico.

BUENO RAMÍREZ, P., JIMÉNEZ SANZ, P.J. & BARROSO BERMEJO, R. 1995: "Prehistoria Reciente en

---

[3] I am not defending the presence of Mesolithic pottery, in the way that it was published for Verdelpino cave (Moure & Fernández-Miranda 1977) and recently proposed for certains level of Mendandia (Alday 2006). I am just stressing the possibility that some regional decorative pottery styles could be understand as interpretative trends of local previous traditions.

el Noroeste de la provincia de Guadalajara", en Balbín, R., Valiente, J. & Mussat, M. T. (coord.): *Arqueología en Guadalajara*, Alicante: 71-95.

BUGOCKI, P. 2003: Neolithic Dispersals in Riverine Interior Central Europe, in Ammerman, A. J & Biagi, P. (Ed): *The Widening Harvest. The Neolithic Transition in Europe: Looking Back, Looking Forward.* Colloquia and Conference Papers, 6, Archaeological Institute of America: 249-272.

CALADO, M. 2000: Neolitização e megalitismo no Alentejo central: uma lectura espacial, *Neolitização e megalitismo da Península Ibérica,* Actas do 3° Congresso de Arqueología Peninsular, Vol. III. Oporto: 35-45.

CANALS, A., SAUCEDA, I. y CARBONELL, E. 2004: The project the first settlers in Extremadura and the Palaeolithic in the Salor area, *Acts of XIVth U.I.S.P.P.* British Archaeological Reports: 157-167

CERRILLO CUENCA, E. 1999: La cueva de El Conejar (Cáceres): avance al estudio de las primeras sociedades productoras en la penillanura cacereña, *Zephyrus* LII: 107-128.

CERRILLO CUENCA, E. 2005: *Los primeros grupos neolíticos de la cuenca extremeña del Tajo.* British Archaeological Reports, S 1393. Oxford.

COLLADO GIRALDO, H. 2005: Un nuevo ciclo de arte prehistórico en Extremadura: el arte rupestre de las sociedades de economía recolectora durante el Holoceno inicial como precedene del arte rupestre en Extremadura, In Calado, M. (Ed.) *Sinais da Pedra . Actas do 1° Colóquio Internacional sobre Megalitismo e Arte Rupestre na Europa Atlântica.* Évora, Fundação Eugénio de Almeida (CD-Rom electronic edition).

DELIBES, G. & ZAPATERO, P. 1996: "De lugar de habitación a sepulcro monumental: una reflexión sobre la trayectoria del yacimiento neolítico de La Velilla, en Osorno (Palencia)", *I Congrés del Neolític a la Península Ibérica*, Rubricatum, 1, Vol 1: 337-348.

DÍAZ del RÍO, P. & CONSUEGRA, S. 1999: Primeras evidencias de estructuras de habitación y almacenaje neolíticas en el entorno de la campiña madrileña: el yacimiento de "La Deseada" (Rivas-Vaciamadrid, Madrid), *II Congrés del Neolític a la Península Ibérica.* Sagvntvm-PLAV, Extra-2: 251-257.

DINIZ, M. 2003: O Neolítico antigo do interior alentejano: lecturas a partir do sítio de Valada do Mato (Évora), In Gonçalves, V. dos S. (ed.): *Muita gente, poucas antas? Origens, espaços e contextos do Megalitismo. Actas do II Coloquio Internacional sobre Megalitismo*, Trabalhos de Arqueología 25: 57-80.

ESTREMERA PORTELA, M.S. 2003: *Primeros agricultores y ganaderos en la Meseta Norte: el Neolítico de la Cueva de La Vaquera (Torreiglesias, Segovia),* Arqueología en Castilla y León, 11. Zamora.

FERNÁNDEZ-POSSE M. D. 1980: Los materiales de la Cueva del Aire (Patones, Madrid), *Noticiario Arqueológico Hispano*, 10: 41-64.

GAVILÁN, B., VERA, J.C., PEÑA CHOCARRO, L. & MÁS CORNELLA, M. 1996: El V° y IV° milenios en Andalucía Central: la cueva de Los Murciélagos de Sueros (Córdoba). Recientes aportaciones, *I Congrés del Neolitic a la Península Ibérica*, Rubricatum 1, vol. 1: 323-327.

GUILAINE, J. & FERREIRA, O. da V. 1970 : Le Neolithique ancien au Portugal, *Bulletin de la Société Préhistorique Française*, t. 67, 1970. Ètudes et travaux, fasc. 1: 304-322.

GUILAINE, J., EVIN, J. & MARTZLUFF, M. 1995: Datacions isotòpiques de les capes 1 a la 6 de la Balma de Margineda. In Guilaine, J. & Martzluff, M. (dirs.) *Les excavacions a la Balma de Margineda (1978-1991).* Vol. I: 91-93.

GUTIÉRREZ, A. 1966: *Miscelánea arqueológica de Diego-Álvaro.* Ávila.

JIMÉNEZ, J. 2005: El proceso de neolitización en la Comunidad de Madrid. In Arias Cabal, P., Ontañón Peredo, R. & García-Moncó Piñeiro, C. (eds): *III Congreso del Neolítico en la Península Ibérica.* Santander: 903-912.

JUAN-CABANILLES, J. & MARTÍ OLIVER, B. 2002: Poblamiento y procesos culturales en la Península Ibérica del VII al V milenio A.C. (8000-5500 BP). Una cartografía de la neolitización, in Badal, E.; Bernabéu, J. & Martí, B. (Eds): *El paisaje en el Neolítico mediterráneo*, Sagvtvm-PLAV, Extra-5: 45-87.

JUAN TRESERRAS, J. & MATAMALA, J.C. 2006: Los Barruecos (Malpartida de Cáceres, Cáceres). Estudio de residuos de procesado de un molino barquiforme. In Cerrillo Cuenca, E. (Coord): *Los Barruecos: primeros resultados sobre el poblamiento neolítico de la cuenca extremeña del Tajo.* Memorias de Arqueología Extremeña, 6: 99-102.

KUNST, M. & ROJO GUERRA, M.A. 1999: El Valle de Ambrona: un ejemplo de la primera colonización Neolítica de las tierras del interior peninsular, *II Congrés del Neolític a la Península Ibérica.* Sagvtvm-PLAV, Extra-2: 259-270.

LÓPEZ SÁEZ, J.A., LÓPEZ GARCÍA, P., LÓPEZ MERINO, L., CERRILLO CUENCA, E., González Cordero, A. y Prada, A. 2005: Prehistoric landscapes in North Extremadura between the VIth and the IVth millenia cal. BC. *Journal of Iberian Archaeology*, 7: 23-35.

MORÍN de PABLOS, J., LÓPEZ RECIO, M., BENITO DÍAZ, L. TAPIAS GÓMEZ, F.J. *et al.* 2006: Los últimos cazadores. Yacimiento epipaleolítico en el enlace de la M-30 con la A-3, *Apuntes de Arqueología*, XXII: 22.

MOURE, A. & FERNÁNDEZ-MIRANDA, M. 1977: El abrigo de Verdelpino (Cuenca), *Trabajos de Prehistoria* 34: 69-81.

MUNICIO, L. 1988: El Neolítico en la Meseta Central española. in López, P. (Coord): *El Neolítico en España*, Madrid: 299-237.

ROJO GUERRA, M.A. & ESTREMERA PORTELA, M.S. 2000: El valle de Ambrona y la cueva de La Vaquera: testimonios de la primera ocupación neolítica en la cuenca del Duero, *Neolitização e megalitismo da Península Ibérica*, Actas do 3º Congresso de Arqueología Peninsular, Vol, III. Oporto: 81-95.

ROJO GUERRA, M.A. & ESTREMERA PORTELA, M.S. 2000: Ambrona 1998. Die neolithische Fundkarte un 14C-Datierungen, *Madrider Mitteilungen*, 41: 1-31.

RODRIGUES, S.M. & ANGELUCCI, D. 2004 New data on the stratigraphy and chronology of the prehistoric site of Prazo (Freixo de Numão), *Revista portuguesa de Arqueologia* vol. 7, n. 1: 39-60.

ROJO GUERRA, M.A., GARRIDO PENA, R., & GARCÍA MARTÍNEZ de LAGRÁN, I. (in this volume): The Ambrona Valley (Soria, Spain): a chronological referente for the first Neolithic occupation of Inner Iberia.

RUBIO, I. & BLASCO, C. 1988-89: 1988-89: Análisis cerámicos de la cueva de La Vaquera (Torreiglesias, Segovia), *Zephyrus* XLII-XLIII: 149-160.

RUBIO, I. & BLASCO, C. 2005: Las primeras dataciones absoluytas para el Neolítico madrileño: los materiales de la Colección Bento. In Arias Cabal, P., Ontañón Peredo, R. & García-Moncó Piñeiro, C. (eds): *III Congreso del Neolítico en la Península Ibérica*. Santander: 919-925.

San VALERO APARISI, J. 1946: El Neolítico español y sus relaciones. Esquema de una tesis doctoral, *Cuadernos de Historia Primitiva*, I: 5-33.

VILLA, M. & ROJAS, J.M. 1996: Aportación al conocimiento del neolítico en la Cuenca Media del Tajo, *I Congrés del Neolitic a la Península Ibérica*, Rubricatum 1, vol. 2: 707-714.

ZILHÃO, J. 1992: *Gruta do Caldeirão. O Neolítico Antigo*. Trabalhos de Arqueología 6. Lisboa

ZILHÃO, J. 2000: From Mesolithic to Neolithic in Iberian Peninsula. In Price, T.D. (ed): *Europe's first farmers*. Cambridge: 144-182.

ZILHÃO, J. 2003: The Neolithic Trasintion in Portugal and the Role of Demic Difusión in the Spread of Agricultura cross West Mediterranean Europe, in Ammerman, A.J & Biagi, P. (Ed): *The Widening Harvest. The Neolithic Transition in Europe: Looking Back, Looking Forward*. Colloquia and Conference Papers, 6, Archaeological Institute of America: 207-222.

ZAPATA, L., PEÑA-CHOCARRO, L., PÉREZ JORDÁ, G. & STIKA, H.P.: Early Neolithic Agriculture in the Iberian Peninsula, *Journal of World Prehistory*, vol. 18, n. 4: 283-325.

NEOLITHISATION ET STRUCTURE SOCIALE: DONNEES ET DISCUSSION DANS LE NORD-EST DE L'ESPAGNE

Xavier CLOP

Departament de Prehistòria. Universitat Autònoma de Barcelona. O8193 Bellaterra (Espagne)

Juan Francisco GIBAJA

Becario postdoctoral da FCT adscrito a la Universidade do Algarve. Faculdade de Ciências Humanas e Sociais, Campus de Gambelas, 8000-117 Faro (Portugal). Colaborador del Museu d'Arqueologia de Catalunya (Barcelona)

E-mail: jfgibaja@ualg.pt

Resumo: O nosso trabalho pretende discutir o que é possível dizer sobre as estruturas sociais dos grupos que protagonizaram o início e desenvolvimento do mode de vida campesino no Nordeste da Península Ibérica. Com efeito, não apresentaremos uma proposta fechada ou um modelo concreto, uma vez que cremos ser mais proveitoso levantar alguns aspectos específicos relevantes para a discussão que propomos. Propomos uma reflexão aberta com a intenção de impulsionar um debate, nem que seja pondo em frente dos investigadores interpretações para se oporem.
Palavras-chave: Neolitização; Estruturas Sociais; Nordeste da Península Ibérica

Résumé: Cet article a pour but d'initier une discussion sur l'analyse de l'organisation sociale des communautés engagées dans le développement de l'économie agricole dans le nord-est de la Péninsule Ibérique. Il ne s'agit pas pour nous de conclure sur le sujet ni même de proposer un modèle concret, mais plutôt d'engager un débat. Ainsi, nous avons choisi d'éclairer un aspect spécifique, en soumettant aux chercheurs et à l'épreuve des faits des interprétations auxquelles se confronter.
Mots-clé: Neolithisation; Organisation Sociale; nord-est de la Péninsule Ibérique

LA PROBLEMATIQUE SUR LA TABLE

La recherche sur le développement du mode de vie paysanne au nord-est de la Péninsule Ibérique a eu un important développement les dernières trente années. Toutefois, un des aspects moins abordés par la recherche a été l'étude de leurs structures sociales. Mais connaître les relations sociales développées dans un certain contexte historique doit être un objectif primordial si on veut comprendre les processus développés par les communautés étudiés et les causes et les conséquences des changements du registre archéologique.

Nous voulons poser la discussion sur les structures sociales des premiers groupes paysannes du nord-est de la Péninsule Ibérique, en effectuant une réflexion ouverte avec l'intention de promouvoir ce débat, ni qui est en proposant des interprétations à auxquelles s'opposer.

Les sociétés néolithiques ont basé leur structure économique à la production d'aliments, ce qui diminuait des risques dans l'obtention des ressources subsistenciales. Les processus productifs développés permettent qu'à un plus grand travail investi plus grand ce soit le volume de la production et la capacité de reproduction sociale. On établit maintenant de nouveaux types de relation avec les moyens de production. Ceci favorise le surgissement de la propriété communale des moyens de production, que produit une plus grande richesse matérielle qu'on peur redistribuer et accumuler. La valeur accumulable de la production rend propice un accès différencié aux sources de richesse, en renforçant la hiérarchisation sociale et en favorisant la compétitivité intra et intergroupale. Pour que ceci ait du succès est nécessaire développer une

justification idéologique qui permette de passer de l'effort minimal et la non accumulation à l'exaltation du travail et la nécessité d'accumulation, de reproduction et de particularisation de la propriété. Le développement de tout ce processus peut se refléter, par exemple, dans la différente complexité des mobiliers funérarires ou dans l'inégale quantité de travail investi dans sa réalisation, qui suggèrent l'existence de différences sociales qui pourraient finalement être perpétuées au moyen de lignées.

La valeur accumulable de la production a rendu possible, comme ont proposé déjà d'autres auteurs, le surgissement de la "richesse". La valeur accumulable est le résultat de la dynamique productive et prédictive de l'économie agricole, qui finit par produire une certaine accumulation de biens (Testart, 2005, 2006).

Un travail ethnologique comparatif souligne que les chasseurs-cuilleurs et les horticulteurs avec peu de stockage ne recourent pas au gaspillage de biens dans leurs obligations sociales. Même s'il y a un certain type de "richesse" est peu développée et on ne l'utilise pas dans les principales stratégies sociales inter et intragroupales. Au contraire et avec peu d'exceptions, les sociétés paysannes avec stockage sont sociétés avec "richesse" qui l'utilisent dans beaucoup d'occasions sociales: achat de l'épouse, paiement du prix du sang, sanctions, etc. L'ethnologie montre en outre que les sociétés actuelles du type néolithique ne sont pas seulement "riches" mais aussi il y a des différences internes selon la "richesse".

Sur ces bases théoriques et d'appui dans le registre ethnographique, nous pouvons proposer que le Néolithique a été marqué, entre d'autres caractéristiques, par l'apparition de la "richesse" et, surtout, parce que la "richesse" a été depuis ce moment un facteur clef de la vie sociale, puisqu'elle faut payer dans chaque grande occasion sociale et parce que toutes les structures sociales sont dorénavant inséparables de cette nouvelle donnée. En définitive, si les sociétés néolithiques ont été marquées par l'apparition de la "richesse" on peut penser qu'ils les ont aussi été, évidemment, par la différenciation sociale entre des individus "riches" et "pauvres".

La vision plus commune sur les premières communautés paysannes du nord-est de la Péninsule Ibérique est qu'elle s'agit de groupes familiaux autosuffisants avec une structure sociale égalitaire, où la population féminine et les jeunes individus ont une position inférieure en relation aux adultes masculins. Mais, globalement, la cohérence du groupe doive d'être haute (Molist, 2005).

LES PRATIQUES FUNERAIRES AU NORD-EST DE LA PENINSULE IBERIQUE

Nous ne savons rien sur les pratiques funéraires des premières communautés paysannes du VI millénaire. Ce vide archéologique permet de poser différentes hypothèses: a) le hasard a fait qu'on n'ait pas trouvé ces enterrements; b) le traitement funéraire n'est pas reflété dans le registre archéologique; c) les premières sociétés paysannes ne sont suffisamment développées pour devoir démontrer ni la "richesse" ni le rôle de leurs individus dans le contexte de leurs processus de reproduction sociale.

Les pratiques funéraires sont bien développées depuis la fin du VI millénaire, avec l'utilisation des grottes et abris et la construction de différents types de structures funéraires qui reflètent, en toute sécurité, d'importants changements dans l'organisation sociale, économique et politique. Il faut souligner qu'il y a aussi des dépôts collectifs comme des dépôts individuels.

À la fin du VI millénaire et pendant la V millénaire on utilise des grottes comme niches funéraires: Cova dels Avellaners (Bosch et Tarrús, 1991), Cova del Pasteral (Bosch, 1986), Cova de Les Grioteres (Castany, 1992), Cova dels Lladres (Ten, 1980). Sont toujours des inhumations primaires successives qui forment dépôts collectifs. Le mobilier est formé par céramique, faune et ornements. Il faut souligner le cas de els Avellaners, un des dépôts funéraires collectifs plus vieilles de l'Europe. Il y avait trois petites cellules d'inhumation avec les restes de demi douzaine d'individus dans chacune de d'elles, en y ayant un nombre minimal de 19 individus (avec 6 enfants et 1 adolescent).

Il y a aussi dans la côte centrale catalane les premières nécropoles au plain air, avec tombes avec inhumation individuelle ou double, comme Sant Pau du Camp (24 unités sépulcrales) ou l'Hort d'en Grimau (5 unités sépulcrales) (Mestres, 1988-1989; Granados et al., 1991). Dans les tombes, couvertes avec une accumulation de pierres, le corps est fléchi et repose sur le côté gauche. Le mobilier est formé par céramiques, industrie lithique en silex, petites haches polies, moulins et ornements personnels (Fig. 4.1 et 4.2).

Dans le sud de la côte catalane, dans l'embouchure de l'Ebre, ont a enterrements isolés et nécropoles parmi 2 et 11 structures funéraires. Sont des tombes avec un individu accompagné de récipients céramiques, industrie lithique comptes, brassards ou restes de faune. Sa chronologie est établie par le parallèle avec les matériaux de l'habitat proche du Barranc d'en Fabra, dont la date est 4900-4650 BC (Bosch et al., 1996).

Apparaissent aussi maintenant, dans le Prepyrenée catalan, les premières mégalithiques: les chambres néolithiques avec tumulus complexe (Cruells et al., 1992). Le "Groupe de Tavertet" est formé par 7-8 sepultures dans un secteur de 2 km de diamètre. Il s'agit de grandes constructions, avec un grand tumulus de terre (diamètre maximal de 22 m ; hauteur maximale 2 m) avec une couronne extérieure en pierre sèche. La chambre funéraire, de dalles, est quadrangulaire. Les inhumations sont individuelles et primaires. Le cadavre est fléchi. Le mobilier est semblable à ce qui est déjà cité, mais avec des vases de type Montboló et outillage de silex melado. La chronologie absolue mis sa construction et utilisation dans la dernière part du VI et pendant toute le V millénaire BC. Face au reprofitement des grottes ou à la facilité relative d'enterrer dans fosses, les structures mégalithiques reflètent un haut investissement de travail en bénéfice de certains individus, qu'on veut aussi dans la même construction de l'enceinte sépulcrale comme dans quelques objets déposés, comme les éléments de silex "melado" d'origine probablement étrangère.

Entre la fin du V et les débuts du IV millénaire BC on entame la construction et l'utilisation des sepulcres à couloir. Une intéressante proposition récente propose que ces mégalithes soient à l'origine structures funéraires individuelles qui sont réutilisées postérieurement comme sépulcres collectives. Cette suggestive idée a besoin toutefois de vérification empirique.

Au début du IV millénaire, on abandonne totalement l'utilisation des grottes. Maintenant, outre les sépulcres à couloir, dans les pratiques funéraires on utilisera les connues sepulcros de fosa dans partir centrale de la côte et du prelitoral et les cistes dans la Dépression Centrale Catalane.

Les sepulcros de fosa sont structures d'inhumation individuelle et primaire, situés préférentiellement dans zones plaines et vallées et forment grands nécropoles organisme (Bòbila Madurell: quelque 130 enterrements), nécropoles plus petits (Camí de Can Grau, Pla del Riu de les Marcetes) ou sont des structures iso-

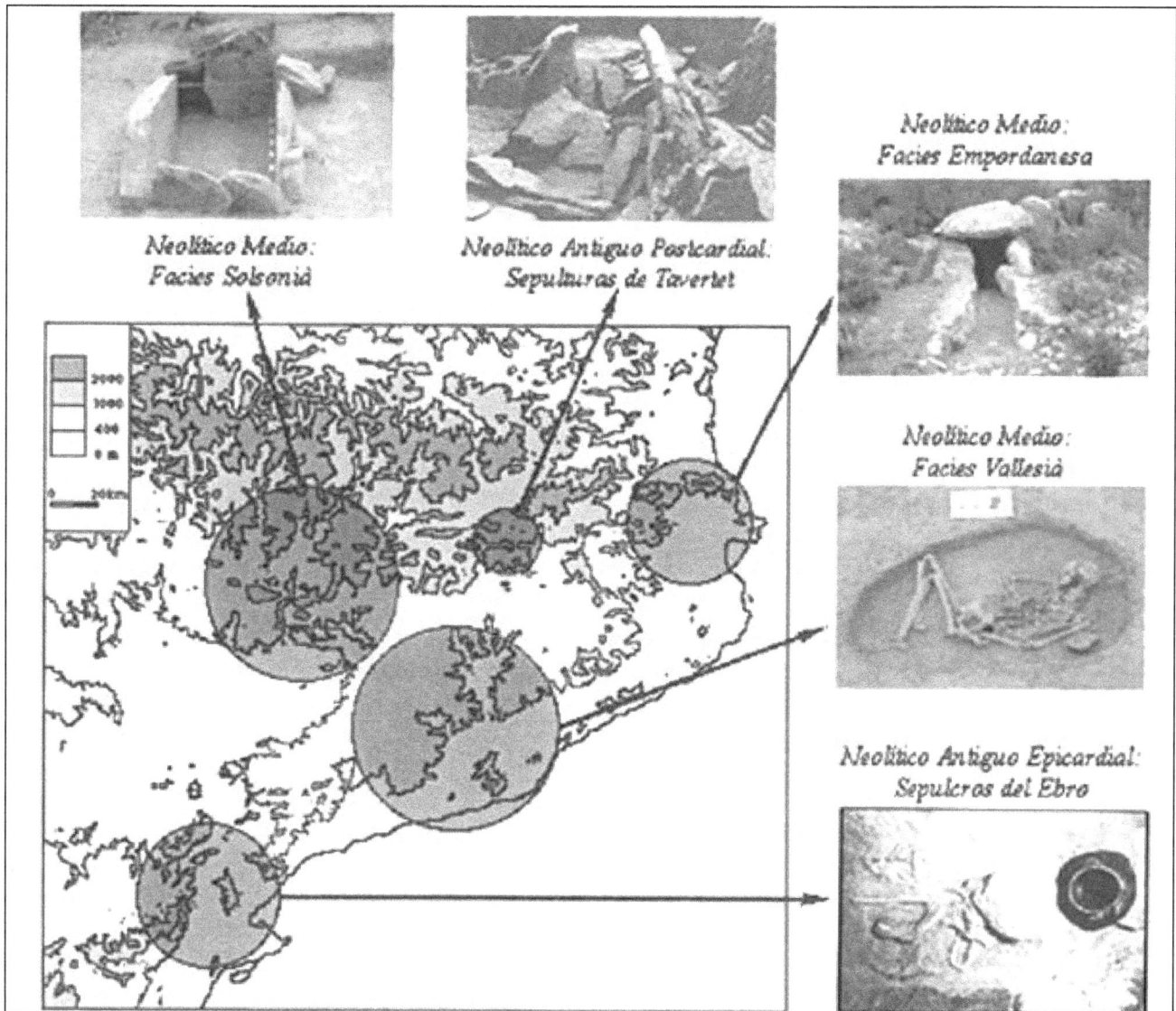

Fig. 4.1. Pratiques funéraires néolithiques dans le nord-est de la Péninsule ibérique

lées (Pou *et al.* 1996; Guitart 1987; Gibaja 2003) (Fig. 4.3).

Bien qu'on à laisser le même type de mobilier, il y a certaines différences significatives avec ce qui est les structures du V millénaire, comme l'outillage élaboré dans "silex melado", des instruments polis effectués avec des lithologies probablement étrangères (serpentina ou jadeita), nombreux ornements élaborés dans variscita des mines de Gavà, etc.

Avec ces différences qualitatives il y a aussi qui sont quantitatifs. Est révélateur la présence d'inhumations dont les matériaux associés ressortent par leur quantité et qualité. Bien que dans les enterrements de cette période il soit habituel qui il n'y a rien ou peu matériel (0-10 effectifs), il y a sépulcres qui rompent avec cette règle: certaines tombes de la Bòbila Madurell, Bòbila d'en Joca... L'étude réalisée par un de nous a démontré tant l'existence de différences qualitatives et quantitatives

statistiquement significatives entre unes et d'autres individus. La présence d'individus très jeunes avec mobiliers considérés d'une plus grande valeur, permet de poser que maintenant le "lieu social" peut déjà être acquis par héritage (Gibaja 2003).

REFLEXION SUR LA PROBLEMATIQUE PRESENTE

En définitive, l'évaluation en termes de structure sociale des dépôts funéraires des premiers paysans du nord-est de la Péninsule Ibérique nous permet proposer cette hypothèse de travail:

1. Il n'y a pas certitude que les communautés paysannes du VI millénaire aient des inégalités sociales internes, au-delà de ce qui est probables par sexe et âge, ce qui peut être interprété de différentes manières, bien qu'une de d'elles soit que le développement du système paysan n'a pas donné lieu encore à la nécessité

Fig. 4.2. Sépulture individuelle de la nécropole
de Sant Pau del Camp (Barcelone)

Fig. 4.3. Sépulture individuelle de la nécropole
de Bòbila Madurell (Barcelone)

de recourir aux pratiques funéraires comme une forme d'expression du système reproduction et organisation sociale;

2. À la fin du VI millénaire et pendant la première moitié du V, l'accumulation de la "richesse" qui entraîne le développement du mode de vie paysan et les contradictions intragroupales et intergroupales ont recouru aux pratiques funéraires comme un complexe forme d'expression de toute cette accumulation d'éléments. La résolution n'a pas été identique dans toutes les communautés, si qui au moins il y a eu deux voies:

a) communautés avec un plus petit degré d'inégalités internes, dans lesquelles les individus sont enterrés dans des dépôts collectifs qui expriment tant l'appartenance à un certain groupe comme le droit utilisation et exploitation d'un territoire spécifique;

b) dans certains groupes on développe l'inhumation individuelle d'individus masculins, avec un important investissement de travail social ou dans l'architecture ou dans la valeur de certains éléments matériels déposés avec eux. Ceci "droit" ne serait pas probablement héréditaire. Nous ne connaissons pas les pratiques funéraires du reste de la communauté;

3. pendant la seconde moitié du V millénaire, on étend le droit à l'enterrement individuel aux hommes, femmes et enfants du groupe. Dans certaines structures on observe des caractéristiques particulières qui peuvent indiquer le rôle social différent que pourraient avoir ces individus.

4. À partir du IV millénaire, les enterrements individuels deviennent la pratique habituelle. Les mobiliers permettent d'établir qu'il existe maintenant de différences internes claires, tant en sens horizontal comme en sens vertical et qu'existe une transmission par héritage du lieu social, comme le démontrent certains enterrements d'individus infantiles d'âge jeune.

Dans notre hypothèse, par conséquent, on pose que le processus d'inégalité sociale s'initie dans le nord-est de la Péninsule Ibérique, au moins depuis la fin du VI millénaire, en n'y ayant pas un seul schéma de relations si qui il y a, au moins, deux. Cette dualité serait maintenue le long de la V millénaire avec une extension progressive de la nécessité sociale de distinguer aux individus, processus qui terminera pendant le IV millénaire avec le développement de relations sociales clairement inégales tant en sens horizontal comme vertical.

La connaissance des caractéristiques sociales des premières communautés paysannes constitue, à notre avis, un aspect clef pour comprendre comment et de quelle manière a eu lieu son développement. Comme nous avons dit, notre de proposition est limité à une zone très concrète. Toutefois, la nécessité de poser ces questions doit être étendue à d'autres zones où le développement de la recherche a augmenté de manière très remarquable le registre disponible durant ces dernières années. En ce sens, par exemple, les discussions maintenues pendant les dernières années autour du développement des structures sociales dans le cadre "du néolithique rubané" nous paraissent hautement positives et stimulantes. Avec notre proposition, nous voulons seulement proposer hypothèse sur cette importante question pour développer des travaux dans notre zone d'étude qui permet de les contraster ou de les réfuter et, de manière plus générale, d'examiner et d'avancer dans la connaissance des caractéristiques socio-économiques et idéologiques générales des premières sociétés paysannes.

Bibliographie

BOSCH, A. (1986) – La cova del Pasteral. Un jaciment neolític a la vall mitjana del Ter. *Quaderns del Centre d'Estudis Comarcals de Banyotes. Homenatge al Dr. Joseph m^a Corominas.* Banyoles (Barcelona). II, p. 71-80.

BOSCH, A.; TARRÚS, J. (1991) – *La cova sepulcral del Neolític antic de l'Avellaner, Cogolls, Les Planes d'Hostoles (La Garrotxa).* Girona, Sèrie Monogràfica 11, Centre d'Investigacions Arqueològiques, 142 p.

BOSCH, J.; FORCADELL, A.; VILLALBÍ, M.M. (1996) – El "Barranc d'en Fabra": asentamiento de inicios del IV milenio a.C. en el curso inferior del Ebro. *I Congrés del Neolític a la Península Ibèrica, Rubricatum.* Barcelona. 1, p. 391-395.

CASTANY, J. (1992) – Montboló i Chassey a Grioteres: Vilanova de Sau, Osona. Estratigrafia, paleoecologia, paleoeconomia i datació. *Estat de la Investigació sobre el Neolític a Catalunya, 9è Col.loqui International d'Arqueologia de Puigcerdà.* Puigcerdà. p. 150-152.

CRUELLS, W.; CASTELLS, J.; MOLIST, M. (1992) – Una necròpolis de "cambres amb túmul complex" del IV mil.leni a la Catalunya interior. *Estat de la Investigació sobre el Neolític a Catalunya, 9è Col.loqui International d'Arqueologia de Puigcerdà.* Puigcerdà. p. 244-248.

GIBAJA, J.F. (2003) – *Comunidades Neolíticas del Noreste de la Península Ibérica. Una aproximación socio-económica a partir del estudio de la función de los útiles líticos.* BAR International Series S1140, Oxford, 318 p.

GRANADOS, O.; PUIG, F.; FARRÉ, R. (1991) – La intervenció arqueològica a Sant Pau del Camp: un nou jaciment prehistòric al Pla de Barcelona. *Tribuna d'Arqueologia.* Barcelona.1990-1991, p. 27-32.

GUITART, I. (1987) – La necrópolis neolítica del Pla del Riu de les Marcetes (Manresa, Bages). *Tribuna d'Arqueologia.* Barcelona 1986-1987, p. 41-47.

MESTRES, J. (1988/1989) – Les sepultures neolítiques de l'Hort d'en Grimau (Castellví de la Marca, Alt Penedès). *Olerdulae, Revista del Museu de Vilafranca.* Vilafranca del Penedès. 1-4, p. 97-129.

MOLIST, M. (2005) – Les primeres societats pageses. *In* AA. VV. (2005) *Història agrària dels Països Catalans* I. Antiguitat: pp. 103-178; 1ª edició; Universitats dels Països Catalans, Barcelona.

POU, R.; MARTÍ, M.; BORDAS, A.; DÍAZ, J.; MARTÍN, A. (1996) – La cultura de los "Sepulcros de Fosa" en el Vallès. Los yacimientos de "Bòbila Madurell" y "Camí de Can Grau" (St. Quirze del Vallès y la Roca del Vallès -Barcelona-). *I Congrés del Neolític a la Península Ibèrica, Rubricatum.* Barcelona. 1, p. 519-526.

TEN, R. (1980) – Notes entorn del neolític vallesà. *Arraona.* Sabadell. 10, p. 6-25.

TESTART, A. (2005) – *Eléments de classification des sociétés.* Éditions Errance. París, 160 p.

TESTART, A. (2006) – Comment concevoir une collaboration entre anthropologie sociale et archéo-logie? À quel prix? Et pourquoi?. Bulletin de la Société Préhistorique Française. Paris. 103/2, p. 385-398.

EL VALLE DE AMBRONA (SORIA, ESPAÑA): UN REFERENTE CRONOLÓGICO PARA LA PRIMERA OCUPACIÓN NEOLÍTICA DEL INTERIOR PENINSULAR

Manuel A. ROJO-GUERRA
Universidad de Valladolid

Rafael GARRIDO-PENA, Íñigo GARCÍA-MARTÍNEZ-de-LAGRÁN
ARCADIA (Instituto de Promoción Cultural), FUNGE, Universidad de Valladolid

Abstract: The Ambrona Valley (Soria, Spain): a chronological reference for the first Neolithic occupation of Inner Iberia.
The ample set of absolute dates, both on charcoal and short life samples (fauna, cereals), obtained in two open air settlements (La Lámpara and La Revilla) suggest a review of the chronological framework attributed to the first Neolithic colonization of Iberia. They also ask us to deeply reflect on the functioning of these habitats from the first communities with productive economies in the interior of Iberia, and on the limits and problems of the ^{14}C method application. Chronologies have been traditionally built on the basis of a single date or a reduced set of dates on each site, when the availability of ample sets of dates from the same structure (number 4 of La Revilla and 9 of La Lámpara, for instance) occasionally offers surprisingly big temporal spans, and shows that the matter is much more complex than what was thought until the present day.
Key Words: ^{14}C, Early Neolithic, settlements, pits, Inner Iberia

Resumo: O extenso conjunto de datações absolutas obtidas, quer sobre carvão quer sobre amostras de vida curta (fauna, cereais), em dois habitats ao ar livre (La Lámpara e La Revilla) permitem rever o esquema cronológico construído para a primeira colonização neolítica da Península Ibérica.
Em simultâneo, este conjunto permite discutir as modalidades de funcionamento dos habitats das primeiras comunidades produtoras no interior peninsular, e os limites e problemas da datação por ^{14}C.
Ao contrário das cronologias tradicionalmente estabelecidas, a partir de uma data ou de um pequeno conjunto de datas de diferentes sítios, o amplo conjunto de datações obtida numa mesma estrutura (como por exemplo na nº 4 de La Revilla e na nº9 de La Lámpara), demonstrou um período de utilização das mesmas inesperadamente amplo e permitiu detectar uma complexidade nos cenários de uso de estruturas domésticas anteriormente desconhecida.
Palavras-chave: ^{14}C; Neolítico antigo; habitats; estruturas negativas; Interior peninsular

INTRODUCCIÓN

El Valle de Ambrona se sitúa en el sureste de la provincia de Soria, en el entronque de los sistemas Ibérico y Central, a 1100 msnm (Figura 5.1). Presenta en su configuración geológica distintas unidades geomorfológicas: las superficies de erosión del páramo (calizas, dolomías, carniolas y margas), que en la actualidad son, en su mayoría, terrenos incultos, aprovechados como pastos. El fondo del Valle, que presenta en torno a su eje fluvial depósitos holocenos de origen aluvial y, en sus límites exteriores, afloramientos de la facies Keuper, que forman el glacis entre la paramera y el fondo del Valle. Aquí es donde hoy en día encontramos la mayoría de las tierras de labor.

Además, nuestra área de estudio es una zona de drenaje indeciso de las aguas superficiales, lo que favorece la creación de humedales y lagunas, de las cuales en la actualidad sólo se mantiene activa la Laguna de La Sima, mientras que las de Ambrona y Conquezuela, artificialmente drenadas, sólo recuperan ocasionalmente parte de su actividad (Figura 5.1).

Se trata de un punto de paso estratégico, situado en la divisoria entre tres de las principales cuencas hidrográficas de la Península (Duero, Ebro y Tajo), razón que podría explicar la extraordinaria densidad de yacimientos arqueológicos, que supera en la actualidad el centenar de estaciones prehistóricas (Rojo y Kunst 1999a). Desde hace diez años se viene desarrollando en este ámbito el "Plan Integral de Actuación en el Valle de Ambrona", un ambicioso proyecto de investigación multidisciplinar que hemos acometido desde la Universidad de Valladolid y el Instituto Arqueológico Alemán de Madrid (Kunst y Rojo 2000; Rojo 1999; Rojo y Kunst 1996, 1999a, 1999b, 1999c, 1999d, 2002; Rojo, Kunst, Garrido, García y Morán, 2005), y que tiene como objetivo primordial el estudio de la implantación de las primeras comunidades agrícolas en el sector suroriental de la Meseta Norte. En este contexto se han desarrollado diversas excavaciones y prospecciones, que han documentado multitud de yacimientos prehistóricos de gran interés, entre los cuales se encuentran los que aquí analizaremos más detalladamente: La Lámpara y La Revilla del Campo.

LOS YACIMIENTOS: LA LÁMPARA Y LA REVILLA, EN AMBRONA

La Lámpara

El yacimiento se sitúa en el sector inferior de la ladera norte de Sierra Ministra, en el extremo suroccidental de la localidad de Ambrona, en la margen derecha del río

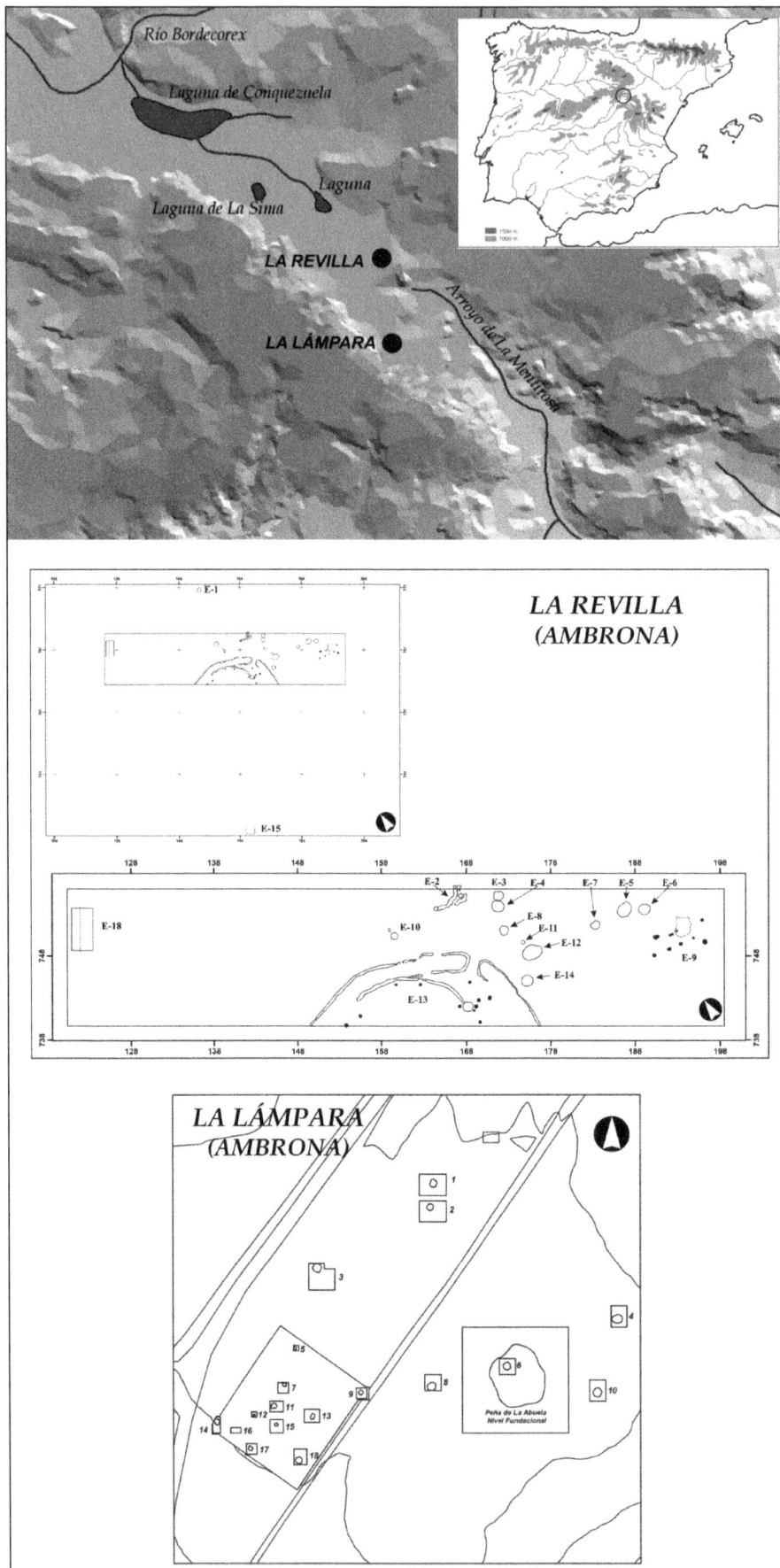

Fig. 5.1. Localización de los yacimientos de La Revilla del Campo y La Lámpara en Ambrona (Soria). Planta de las estructuras excavadas en La Lámpara. Planta de las estructuras excavadas en La Revilla del Campo

Masegar/Arroyo de La Mentirosa, a unos 650 m del cauce, ocupando una superficie muy amplia (unas 13 Has.), que va desde las plataformas inferiores de la ladera hasta las tierras de labor que se extienden por la zona llana, a ambos lados de la Cañada Real Soriana Oriental (Fig. 5.1).

Se compone de los típicos hoyos, característicos de buena parte de los asentamientos prehistóricos de La Meseta. Los 18 que fueron excavados proporcionaron materiales arqueológicos de gran interés, como cerámicas lisas y decoradas, e industria lítica tallada en sílex y pulimentada, así como restos paleobotánicos, fundamentalmente de cereales, y faunísticos, sobre todo domésticos (ovicápridos entre ellos). Todos ellos permiten identificar el sitio como un importante lugar de hábitat neolítico con una agricultura y ganadería perfectamente establecidas. A ello hay que añadir la localización de un enterramiento individual en fosa (hoyo 1), de una mujer de avanzada edad, que estaba acompañada de un rico ajuar funerario, con cerámicas decoradas incisas e impresas, y que ha sido datada por C14 a finales del VI milenio cal AC (Rojo y Kunst 1996; 1999a; 1999c; 1999d; Kunst y Rojo 2000).

Se han datado 24 muestras de este yacimiento pertenecientes a siete hoyos distintos, 17 de ellas sobre muestras de carbón, seis de hueso y una de cereales. Sólo hemos de excluir del análisis tres dataciones que consideramos claramente ajenas al contexto neolítico estudiado:
KIA16582. 9085±50 BP. 2 Sigma cal AC 8449-8214, y KIA16573. 7108±34 BP. 2 Sigma cal AC 6053-5890 procedentes de los hoyos 7 y 16 respectivamente, que no proporcionaron material arqueológico alguno.
KIA16572. 8376±36 BP. 2 Sigma cal AC 7540-7328, del hoyo 11, donde se recuperaron pocos materiales arqueológicos, y otra fecha realizada sobre muestra de hueso, perfectamente acorde con el margen crono-lógico mejor representada en la amplia serie de dataciones disponible para este yacimiento (KIA 21348. 6125±33. 2 Sigma cal AC 5209 – 4861).

Teniendo en cuenta todas las fechas obtenidas en las distintas estructuras excavadas de La Lámpara, a excepción de las mencionadas, se puede deducir que este asentamiento estuvo ocupado por grupos humanos neolíticos, con una agricultura y ganadería perfectamente asentadas, de forma estacional pero continua, a lo largo de la primera mitad del VI milenio cal AC. Entre el 6000-5700 cal AC se construyó y colmató el hoyo 18, y carbones y materiales de esta etapa acabaron rellenando en etapas posteriores (5500-5400 cal AC) el hoyo 9. Entre 5700-5600 no hay testimonio de que se realizara ninguna estructura, pero materiales y carbones de este momento acabaron en el relleno de los hoyos 13 y 9. Finalmente entre 5500-5400 cal AC se construyeron y amortizaron como basureros los hoyos 13 y 9, con materiales propios y también de épocas anteriores. El hoyo 9, aunque realizado y rellenado a mediados del VI milenio cal AC, incorpora materiales y carbones en la tierra con que se

colmata, que representan todos los momentos previos de ocupación del sitio.

Finalmente, no podemos olvidar las fechas hasta ahora disponibles, y ya publicadas (Rojo y Kunst 1999a; 1999c; 1999d; Kunst y Rojo 2000) del enterramiento en fosa de la estructura C de La Lámpara, que situaron esta inhumación y su rico ajuar a finales del VI milenio cal AC. Esto indicaría que, al igual que en el caso de La Revilla, que examinaremos a continuación, la ocupación neolítica del lugar transcurre a lo largo de todo este milenio.

No obstante, hemos de destacar el hecho de que, como ocurre en el resto del Neolítico peninsular (Zilhão, 2001), las seis muestras de vida corta analizadas proporcionan fechas sensiblemente más modernas. Éstas situarían el arranque de la ocupación en torno al 5800-5700 cal AC, y la construcción del hoyo 18 en torno al 5400-5300 cal AC, del hoyo 9 entre el 5300-5200 cal AC, y del 11 en torno al 5200-4900 cal AC. Sin embargo, y lo que es más interesante, las dataciones de La Lámpara siguen siendo muy antiguas dentro del panorama de las muestras de vida corta actualmente disponibles en el Neolítico peninsular, en paralelo con los contextos cardiales más antiguos (5600-5000 cal AC).

Incluso, la fecha KIA 21350 de 6871±33 BP (5808-5706 2 sigma cal AC) es hoy por hoy la más antigua obtenida sobre este tipo de muestras en toda la Península Ibérica, a excepción de las polémicas dataciones de Mendandia (6230-5890 cal AC), donde, a diferencia de nuestro caso, existen niveles mesolíticos bajo los neolíticos y la fauna no es doméstica (Alday 2005).

La Revilla del Campo

El yacimiento de se localiza en la ladera occidental de una de las plataformas inferiores del páramo, que desciende muy tendida, con escasa pendiente (Fig. 5.1), y se extiende por una amplia superficie de unas 18 Has. Se trata, como en el caso de La Lámpara antes comentado, de los típicos hoyos, característicos de los asentamientos prehistóricos de buena parte de La Meseta, y cuya funcionalidad pudo ser diversa (silos, basureros, etc.). La mayor parte de los diez excavados proporcionaron una importante cantidad de materiales arqueológicos de gran interés, como cerámicas lisas y decoradas, e industria lítica pulimentada y tallada en sílex, así como restos faunísticos, que permiten identificarlo, sin ninguna duda, como un importante lugar de hábitat neolítico. Junto a estas estructuras se pudieron documentar otras como dos interesantes y enigmáticos recintos ovales (¿encerraderos para el ganado?, ¿recintos rituales?), realizados a base de una doble zanja donde se encajaban postes de madera, que no se excavaron en su totalidad.

Se han podido datar por C14 34 muestras de este yaci-miento, diez sobre muestras de fauna (tres pertenecientes a ovicápridos), seis de cereales y 18 de carbón, una de las cuales ya fue publicada con anterioridad (KIA-4782: 4750±80 BP, 3701-3352 cal AC, 2 Sigma), que es, además y con diferencia, la datación más moderna (Fig. 5.2).

Teniendo en cuenta en primer lugar las muestras de carbón, tenemos en los hoyos excavados de La Revilla dataciones de C^{14} que sitúan la ocupación de este yacimiento a lo largo de todo el VI milenio cal AC, con algún testimonio aislado de su probable continuación a mediados del V (estructura 8), e incluso hasta mediados del IV (estructura 1). Los testimonios de la ocupación más antigua (6000-5700 cal AC) se dan en las estructuras 4 (dos fechas) y 8 (una fecha), bien es cierto que junto a otras fechas más modernas, que sugieren que estos hoyos se excavaron y amortizaron como basureros posteriormente, incorporando tierra que llevaba en su interior materiales y carbones de la etapa más antigua de utilización del lugar, a comienzos del VI milenio cal AC.

Entre el 5700-5400 cal AC tendríamos fechas en las estructuras 2 (una datación), 4 (dos), 14 (dos), especialmente en este último caso, donde las dos fechas obtenidas sobre muestras de carbón coinciden en situar la construcción y relleno de esta estructura en este periodo cronológico, ya que en los demás tenemos también muestras que ofrecen fechas más antiguas y más modernas. Sin embargo, en este caso las dos fechas obtenidas sobre hueso rebajan esta cronología hasta el último tercio del VI milenio cal AC.

Para el periodo entre 5400-5000 cal AC tenemos fechas en las estructuras 2 (tres dataciones), 4 (cuatro), 8 (una), 14 (dos), 5 (una). En este último caso, dado que se trata de la única fecha disponible podríamos considerar que dataría en este momento, y más concretamente entre 5479-5322 cal AC, la construcción y relleno del hoyo, pero como han demostrado otros hoyos de este yacimiento y del vecino de La Lámpara, antes descrito, disponer de una sola fecha es un procedimiento muy poco fiable para datar una estructura de este tipo. En el caso de las estructuras 2, 4 y 14 es posible que las fechas que se incluyen en este margen cronológico (5470-5301 y 5482-5324 cal AC en el primero, 5475-5316, 5465-5153 cal AC en el segundo, y 5317-5208 y 5388-5296 cal AC, sobre muestra de hueso en el tercero), daten su construcción y relleno, ya que las restantes (5733-5563 cal AC en el primer caso y 6158-5924, 5984-5730, 5733-5559 y 5614-5474 cal AC en el segundo) podrían corresponder a tierra de los alrededores, perteneciente a otras etapas más antiguas de ocupación del yacimiento. La estructura 8 tiene otras dos fechas, una más antigua y otra mucho más moderna (4712-4262 cal AC), que dataría la construcción y relleno de la estructura, nuevamente incorporando tierra con materiales y carbones pertenecientes a etapas de ocupación muy anteriores.

También aquí, como en La Lámpara, se comprueba el notable rejuvenecimiento que experimenta la cronología del sitio cuando se datan muestras de vida corta. Así, las

16 fechas realizadas sobre muestras de fauna (diez) y cereales (seis) sitúan la cronología del yacimiento a lo largo de la segunda mitad del VI milenio cal AC, con una clara concentración de casos en el último tercio del mismo (5300-5000 cal AC). No obstante, las fechas más antiguas se localizan en las estructuras 4, donde también se ubicaban las más elevadas de carbón, con una fecha de fauna doméstica (ovicáprido) (KIA 21356: 5466-5261), 9, con una de cereal (UtC_13347: 5470-5080) y 14, con otra de fauna no identificada (KIA 21358: 5469-5262 cal AC), donde asimismo se documentaban dos fechas sobre carbón de notable antigüedad (5700-5500 cal AC).

PARADOJAS Y PROBLEMAS METODOLÓGICOS DE LA APLICACIÓN DEL MÉTODO DE C^{14}: LA ESTRUCTURA 4 DE LA REVILLA Y EL HOYO 9 DE LA LÁMPARA COMO EJEMPLOS

La disponibilidad de amplias series de dataciones radiométricas en algunas de las estructuras excavadas en estos yacimientos nos ha permitido verificar la existencia de algunos problemas que inciden seriamente en el proceso de datación de las mismas. La notable diferencia existente entre las fechas obtenidas sobre muestras de carbón y las que proceden de otras de vida corta, con ser asimismo desconcertantes y graves, dado que aún suponen la inmensa mayoría de los repertorios de fechas disponibles, es un hecho bien conocido y contrastado (Zilhão 2001). Sin embargo, la amplísima diferencia cronológica existente entre las propias muestras de carbón (un milenio en ocasiones), y no digamos ya de las de vida corta, procedentes de una misma estructura tan elemental como un simple hoyo, que no debió ser utilizado durante mucho tiempo, suponen un reto irresoluble en el estado actual de nuestros conocimientos y arrojan muchas dudas sobre todo el sistema cronológico que se ha construido en torno a los orígenes del Neolítico en la Península Ibérica. Dos ejemplos de nuestros yacimientos sorianos ilustran perfectamente esta cuestión:

La estructura 4 de La Revilla (Figura 5.2A)

Se trata de un hoyo de 180 cm. de diámetro y 86 cm. de profundidad. Los materiales recuperados en esta estructura no son muy abundantes (48 piezas): 24 fragmentos cerámicos y tres elementos líticos, 17 de fauna y restos de carbón. Entre las decoraciones cerámicas destaca la incisión aplicada en líneas horizontales y oblicuas, y las acanaladuras verticales bajo cordón indicado. Se obtuvieron doce fechas de C^{14}, ocho sobre muestras de carbón:

KIA13941. 7165±37 BP. 2 Sigma cal AC 6158 – 5924
KIA13935. 6983±45 BP. 2 Sigma cal AC 5984 – 5730
KIA13939. 6755±57 BP. 2 Sigma cal AC 5733 – 5559
KIA13940. 6568±37 BP. 2 Sigma cal AC 5614 – 5474
KIA13938. 6449±42 BP. 2 Sigma cal AC 5480 – 5320
KIA13942. 6415±36 BP. 2 sigma cal AC 5475 – 5316
KIA13937. 6405±36 BP. 2 Sigma cal AC 5474 – 5304
KIA13936. 6335±46 BP. 2 Sigma cal AC 5465 – 5153

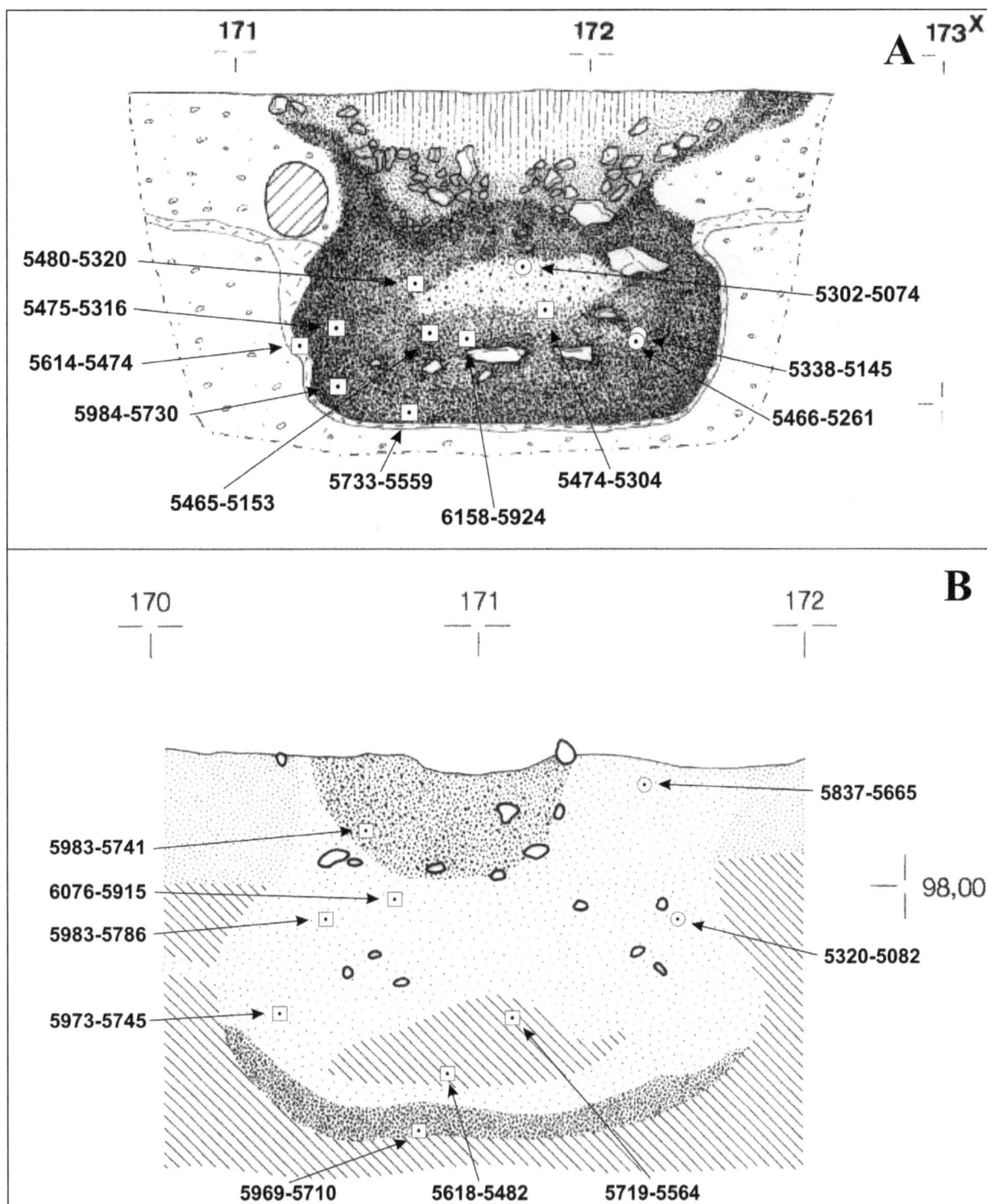

Fig. 5.2. Situación de las muestras datadas por C14 en la estructura 4 de La Revilla del Campo (Ambrona) (A); y en el hoyo 9 de La Lámpara (Ambrona) (B)

Otras tres fechas sobre muestras de hueso:
KIA21351. 6289±31 BP. Fragmento de diáfisis de radio de mesomamífero. 2 Sigma cal AC 5338-5145.
KIA21356. 6355±30 BP. Fragmento de diáfisis de tibia de ovicáprido. 2 Sigma cal AC 5466-5261.
KIA21359. 6245±34. Mandíbula de Sus sp. 2 Sigma cal AC 5302-5074

Se pudieron recuperar 17 fragmentos de fauna, cuatro de ellos pertenecientes a ovicápridos domésticos, y una pelvis de conejo, no pudiéndose identificar los restantes casos con precisión (mesomamíferos y un macromamífero).

En la criba por flotación del sedimento se pudieron identificar restos de cereales domésticos (Triticum monococcum L./dicoccum, Cerealia indet.). Una de estas muestras de cereal se dató: UtC_13348. 6120±60 BP. 2 Sigma cal AC 5260-4850.

Las ocho dataciones sobre muestras de carbón recorren todo el VI milenio cal AC, pero a tramos regulares y de forma perfectamente escalonada, representando así todas las etapas de ocupación del yacimiento. No es razonable atribuir 1000 años de duración a una estructura de este tipo, que se colmataría en unos pocos meses o años, sino que refleja probablemente las actividades desarrolladas en la etapa en que se construyó, 5465-5153 cal AC, según la fecha más moderna disponible, o quizá incluso más tarde si pensamos que también esta muestra fue incorporada en la tierra con que se rellenó el hoyo, que, procedente de los alrededores, representaría en este caso, todas las etapas de ocupación neolítica del sitio a lo largo de todo el VI milenio cal AC.

Si tenemos en cuenta las cuatro muestras de vida corta la cronología se rebajaría hasta el periodo (5466-4850 cal AC), lo cual resulta un hecho bien conocido (Zilhão 2001), pero, nuevamente, el amplio margen de seis siglos que estas muestras también ofrecen resulta sorprendente y desconcertante, si tenemos en cuenta que nos encontramos ante muestras de vida corta recuperadas en la excavación de un simple hoyo.

Hoyo 9 de La Lámpara (Figura 5.2B)

Hoyo aproximadamente circular, de 140 cm de diámetro y 120 cm de profundidad, del que se dataron hasta nueve muestras:

Siete de carbón:
KIA16576. 7136±33 BP. Madera de pino. 2 Sigma cal AC 6076-5915
KIA16568. 7000±32 BP. Madera sin determinar. 2 Sigma cal AC 5983-5786
KIA16580. 6989±48 BP. Madera de pino. 2 Sigma cal AC 5983-5741
KIA16578. 6975±32 BP. Madera sin determinar. 2 Sigma cal AC 5973-5745
KIA16569. 6920±50 BP. Madera de pino. 2 Sigma cal AC 5969-5710
KIA16575. 6744±33 BP. Madera de pino. 2 Sigma cal AC 5719-5564
KIA16579. 6610±32 BP. Madera de pino. 2 Sigma cal AC 5618-5482

Dos muestras de hueso:
KIA 21350. 6871±33 BP. Fragmento apendicular de macroungulado quemado. 2 Sigma cal AC 5837 - 5665
KIA 21352. 6280±33 BP. Fragmento craneal de mesoungulado con erosiones radiculares. 2 Sigma cal AC 5320 – 5082.

Con 40 piezas, el material arqueológico recuperado en este hoyo no es muy abundante, y consiste básicamente en fragmentos de cerámica, con sólo cuatro piezas de industria lítica y escasos restos óseos de fauna. El material cerámico está compuesto en su mayoría por galbos de los que no se puede extraer ningún tipo de información tipológica, pero también contamos con un asa y varios bordes pertenecientes a grandes vasos de paredes rectas y ligeramente entrantes. Sólo seis fragmentos están decorados mediante acanaladuras y los apliques plásticos (cordones en relieve y un pequeño mamelón).

Sólo se recuperaron cuatro elementos de industria lítica, todos ellos en sílex, entre los que sólo destacaremos la presencia de una lámina simple y un denticulado.

Únicamente se recuperaron dos fragmentos de fauna, que corresponden a sendos mesoungulados sin identificar. En la criba por flotación del sedimento se pudieron identificar restos de cereales domésticos (*Cerealia indet.*).

Las siete fechas sobre muestras de carbón obtenidas se comprenden en un amplio margen de casi 600 años (6076-5482 cal AC), pero, y lo que resulta más desconcertante, las dataciones de muestras de vida corta ofrecen un margen aún mayor, de más de siete siglos (5837-5082 cal AC).

Estos dos ejemplos ilustran de forma evidente que las muestras que contienen los hoyos en los lugares de hábitat prehistóricos pertenecen a periodos cronológicos muy amplios, en absoluto coincidentes con la vida de estas sencillas estructuras. Si descartamos la existencia de problemas internos en el propio método de datación, o circunstancias y alteraciones postdeposicionales que podrían explicar estas anomalías en una estructura pero no en varias pertenecientes a dos yacimientos diferentes, hemos de recurrir a otra explicación.

En nuestra opinión lo más lógico sería suponer que en el proceso de relleno de estos hoyos se incorporasen materiales de cronologías anteriores presumiblemente existentes en las cercanías, y fruto quizás de etapas de ocupación previas del lugar, que son únicamente neolíticas en nuestro caso. En cualquier caso, la paradoja cronológica que estas amplias series de fechas plantean, ponen en cuestión, en primer lugar, el procedimiento que habitualmente se sigue en la datación de este tipo de estructuras, fechando una única muestra por hoyo, o incluso por yacimiento en la mayoría de los casos. Pero, además, demuestran la clara necesidad de datar únicamente muestras de vida corta, cuando ello sea posible, pues el efecto de envejecimiento que introduce el carbón es tan claro y considerable que distorsiona por completo las secuencias cronológicas construidas a partir de la datación de este tipo de muestras.

Sin embargo, y a pesar de que hemos ofrecido nuestra explicación de estas discordancias cronológicas detectadas en las series de fechas obtenidas en estos dos asentamientos sorianos, no dejamos de hacer constar nuestra perplejidad ante tales evidencias que cuestionan seriamente los cimientos fundamentales sobre los que se ha construido la secuencia cronológica de nuestra Prehistoria reciente.

LA NEOLITIZACIÓN DEL VALLE DE AMBRONA EN EL MARCO PENINSULAR

La espectacular serie de fechas radiométricas que aquí ofrecemos no sólo introducen numerosos interrogantes difíciles de resolver en lo relativo a la metodología de datación de los yacimientos, sino también respecto a la antigüedad de la introducción del modo de vida neolítico en la Meseta, y por extensión en la Península Ibérica, cimentadas en las bien conocidas secuencias establecidas en el ámbito costero portugués y levantino (Zilhão, 1993, 2001; Bernabeu, 1996, 2002). Estas fechas y otras aún más sorprendentes y polémicas, como las conocidas de Mendandia (Alday, 2005), cuestionan el límite del 5600 cal AC para la llegada del Neolítico a la Península según las muestras de vida corta (Bernabeu y otros, 1999; Bernabeu, 2002; Zilhão 2001).

Así, contamos con fauna doméstica (ovicáprido) en la estructura 4 de La Revilla que ha ofrecido una fecha de 5466-5261 cal AC, muy en consonancia con muchas de las existentes en contextos cardiales de la periferia mediterránea y atlántica peninsulares sobre muestras de vida corta. Así pues, no sólo la colonización de las tierras del interior peninsular se habría producido de forma casi instantánea, apenas unas pocas décadas tras su eventual llegada a los ámbitos costeros peninsulares, sino que todo el proceso podría ser incluso más antiguo y complejo de lo que pensamos en la actualidad.

Este último hecho vendría necesariamente sugerido por las evidencias proporcionadas por la muestra de hueso del hoyo 9 de La Lámpara (*KIA 21350.* 6871±33 BP. 5837–5665 cal AC), que constituye, hasta el momento, la fecha más antigua realizada sobre fauna de todo el Neolítico peninsular, a excepción de las polémicas de Mendandia (Alday 2005). Éstas últimas pertenecen a una ocupación neolítica sin fauna doméstica, que se encuentra situada estratigráficamente sobre otras ocupaciones mesolíticas, por lo que, a pesar de que su excavador insiste en la fiabilidad total de ambas muestras, siempre puede quedar la duda de que los huesos datados procedan de los niveles mesolíticos. Sin embargo en el caso de La Lámpara tal duda resulta improcedente, ya que no se han encontrado testimonios de ocupación mesolítica en todo el Valle de Ambrona, a pesar de la multitud de prospecciones y excavaciones desarrolladas en los últimos diez años con tal objetivo.

Así pues, contamos con un horizonte neolítico sorprendentemente temprano en Ambrona, representado por la fracción más antigua de las fechas de carbón, pero sobre todo por la muestra de hueso del hoyo 9 de La Lámpara (5837–5665 cal AC), donde además carecemos por completo de cerámicas cardiales. Estas evidencias y

otras dispersas en distintas regiones peninsulares sistemáticamente rastreadas por Alday (2003; 2005: 635-654) podrían ilustrar procesos de neolitización asimismo antiguos, al margen de lo cardial, y quizás conectados con fenómenos semejantes documentados al otro lado de los Pirineos.

Bibliografía

ALDAY RUIZ, A. – 2003. Cerámica neolítica de la región vasco-riojana: base documental y cronológica. *Trabajos de Prehistoria* 60(1): 53-80.

ALDAY RUIZ, A. – 2005. *El campamento prehistórico de Mendandia: ocupaciones mesolíticas y neolíticas entre el 8500 y el 6400 b.p.* Álava. Diputación Foral de Álava.

BERNABEU AUBÁN, J. – 1996. "Indigenismo y Migracionismo. Aspectos de la neolitización en la fachada oriental de la Península Ibérica", *Trabajos de Prehistoria*, 53, nº 2: 37-54.

BERNABEU AUBÁN, J. – 2002. "The social and symbolic context of Neolithization", *El Paisaje en el Neolítico mediterráneo, Saguntum*, Extra-5: 209-233.

BERNABEU, J.; PÉREZ, M. y MARTÍNEZ, R. – 1999. "Huesos, neolitización y Contextos Arqueológicos Aparentes", *II Congreso del Neolítico en la Península Ibérica, Saguntum-Plav*, Extra-2: 589-596.

KUNST, M. y ROJO. M. – 2000. Ambrona 1998. Die neolithische Fundkarte und [14]C- Datierungen. *Madrider Mitteilungen* 41: 1-31.

ROJO GUERRA, M.A. – 1999. Proyecto de Arqueología Experimental. Construcción e incendio de una tumba monumental neolítica a partir de los datos obtenidos en la excavación de La Peña de La Abuela. *Boletín de Arqueología Experimental* 3. Madrid: UAM ediciones: 5-11.

ROJO, M. y KUNST, M. – 1996. Proyecto de colaboración hispano-alemán en torno a la introducción de la neolitización en las tierras del Interior Peninsular: planteamientos y primeros resultados, *Cuadernos de Prehistoria de la Universidad Autónoma de Madrid* 23: 87-113.

ROJO, M. y KUNST, M. – 1999a. Zur Neolithisierung des Inneren der Iberischen Halbinsen. Erste Ergebnisse des interdisziplinären, spanisch-deustchen Forschungsprojekts zur Entwicklung einer prähistorischen Siedlungskammer in der Umgebung von Ambrona (Soria, Spanien). Mainz: *Madrider Mitteilungen* 40: 1-52.

ROJO, M. y KUNST, M. – 1999b. La Peña de la Abuela. Un enterramiento monumental neolítico sellado por la acción del fuego, *Revista de Arqueología* 220: 12-19.

ROJO, M. y KUNST, M. – 1999c. El Valle de Ambrona: un ejemplo de la primera colonización Neolítica de las tierras del Interior Peninsular. *II Congrés del Neolític a la Península Ibérica. Valencia, 7-9 Abril, 1999. Saguntum*, Extra 2: 259-270.

ROJO, M. y KUNST, M. – 1999d. La Lámpara y la Peña de la Abuela. Propuesta secuencial del Neolítico Interior en el ámbito funerario. *II Congrés del Neolític a la Península Ibérica. Valencia, 7-9 Abril, 1999. Saguntum*, Extra 2: 503-512.

ROJO, M. y KUNST, M. – 2002. *Sobre el Significado del Fuego en los Rituales Funerarios del Neolítico.* Valladolid: Studia Archaeologica 91.

ROJO, M., KUNST, M., GARRIDO, R., GARCÍA, I. y MORÁN, G. – 2005. *Un Desafío a la Eternidad. Tumbas Monumentales del Valle de Ambrona (Soria, España).* Junta de Castilla y León, Monografías, 14. Soria.

ZILHÃO, J. – 1993. The spread of agro-pastoral economies across Mediterranean Europe: a view from the Far West, *Journal of Mediterranean Archaeology* 6: 5-63.

ZILHÃO, J. – 2001. Radiocarbon evidence for maritime pioneer colonization at the origins of farming in west Mediterranean Europe. *PNAS (Proceedings of the National Academy of Sciences of the United States of America* 98 (24): 14180-14185.

NEOLITHISATION PROCESS IN LOWER TAGUS VALLEY LEFT BANK: OLD PERSPECTIVES AND NEW DATA

César NEVES, Filipa RODRIGUES
CRIVARQUE, Lda, nam@crivarque.net

Mariana DINIZ
Centro de Arqueologia, Faculdade de Letras, Universidade de Lisboa m.diniz@fl.ul.pt

Abstract: This article presents the main goals of a research project design to study the neolithisation process in lower Tagus valley left bank (NAM project – developed, since 2006, by the Research Department of CRIVARQUE, Lda). This area, occupied by late Mesolithic hunter-gatherers at least until 6300 BP, was traditionally seen as a "no-man's land" during Neolithic period.
Agro-pastoralist communities were settled in nearby Estremadura limestone caves and rock-shelters since 6400 BP and in granitic plains of central Alentejo at least since 6000 BP.
New data brought out by recent works in the area – surveying projects and rescue excavations – have revealed, based upon typological criteria since no absolute date is available for the moment, an Early and Middle Neolithic settlement (Casas Velhas da Coelheira, Vala Real, Monte da Foz I, Moita do Ourives).
Using these, still preliminary, data we will discuss some main cultural and chronological issues linking last hunter-gathered societies and first agropastoralist groups in southern Portugal and connections between littoral and in-land Neolithic communities.
Key-words: Neolithisation process; Lower Tagus valley; Early and Middle Neolithic habitats

Resumo: É objectivo deste artigo apresentar as principais linhas de investigação e os primeiros resultados obtidos no âmbito do projecto NAM (Departamento de Investigação e Divulgação da CRIVARQUE, Lda), criado para estudar o processo de neolitização na margem esquerda do Baixo Tejo. Esta área ocupada por caçadores-recolectores do Mesolítico final, até cerca de 6300 BP, foi tradicionalmente entendida como uma "terra de ninguém" ao longo do Neolítico, dada a quase total ausência de informação acerca das primeiras sociedades agro-pastoris, que no entanto estão atestadas em grutas e abrigos calcários da Estremadura, desde 6400 BP, e nas planícies graníticas do Alentejo central, desde 6000 BP.
Novos dados provenientes de trabalhos de emergência e prospecção superficial revelaram um conjunto de sítios – Casas Velhas da Coelheira, Vala Real, Monte da Foz I, Moita do Ourives – que, de acordo com critérios tipológicos, podem ser enquadrados no Neolítico antigo e médio do Sul do actual território português.
Apesar de preliminar, esta informação permite colocar questões acerca dos mecanismos de neolitização da área, das continuidades e/ou rupturas existentes entre os grupos mesolíticos e estes grupos neolíticos, das relações estabelecidas, ao longo do Neolítico, entre territórios do litoral e do interior.
Em simultâneo, a evolução da paisagem holocénica, na margem esquerda do Baixo Tejo, gera cenários dinâmicos que exigem/justificam soluções culturais específicas que importa caracterizar.
Palavras-Chave: Processo de Neolitização; Baixo vale do Tejo; Habitats do Neolítico antigo e médio

PHYSICAL ENVIRONMENT

The NAM project area is located in Lower Tagus Valley (LVT), matching with Salvaterra de Magos and Benavente districts. Both districts stand in Tagus valley left bank, where Quaternary fluvial deposits dominate marking a strong dissymmetry with lower Tagus right bank were Miocene rocks outcrop (Cabral, 2006, p. 53).

Muge River, on the North, St. Estevão River, on the South, Tagus River on the West, and Hercynian Massif, on the East, limited the research area.

In this area, we can recognize three main geomorphological units: Tagus alluvial plain – ranging from two to 13 km width, Quaternary terraces – ranging from Q1 to Q4, and Mio-Pliocene deposits of Tagus Tertiary basin, with fluvial erosion and deposition, eustatic movements and tectonic activity being the main geomorphic processes.

The landscape is characterized by a vast plain with elevations ranging from sea level, in the alluvial plain, to 80 m in Q1 and in Mio-Pliocene deposits.

Muge, Sorraia e St. Estevão/Almansor Rivers are the main tributaries streams of Lower Tagus left bank drainage basin, with a general E-W orientation.

Since the first half of the Holocene, Mediterranean climatic conditions are established in the area with salt marsh vegetation near water courses and *Quercus ilex*, *Juniper*, *Arbutus*, *Vitis vinifera* and *Olea europea* (Azevêdo *et al.*, 2006, p. 69) more in-land.

The Holocene evolution of the landscape is strongly marked by changes in sea level – due to post-glacial transgression – that set Tagus estuary further in-land then today. Salty waters and tide effects reached, at least, Muge River, and some foraminifers from Entre Valas core (Santarém) reveal that sporadically marine or brackish water could reach the place during the first half of the Holocene (Azevêdo *et al.*, 2006, p. 13).

The entire region was in the first half of the Holocene very different from nowadays. This is a picture hard to capture since Tagus flood regime (recorded at least since 8540-8110 BC (Benito, 2006, p. 35), lateral migration of

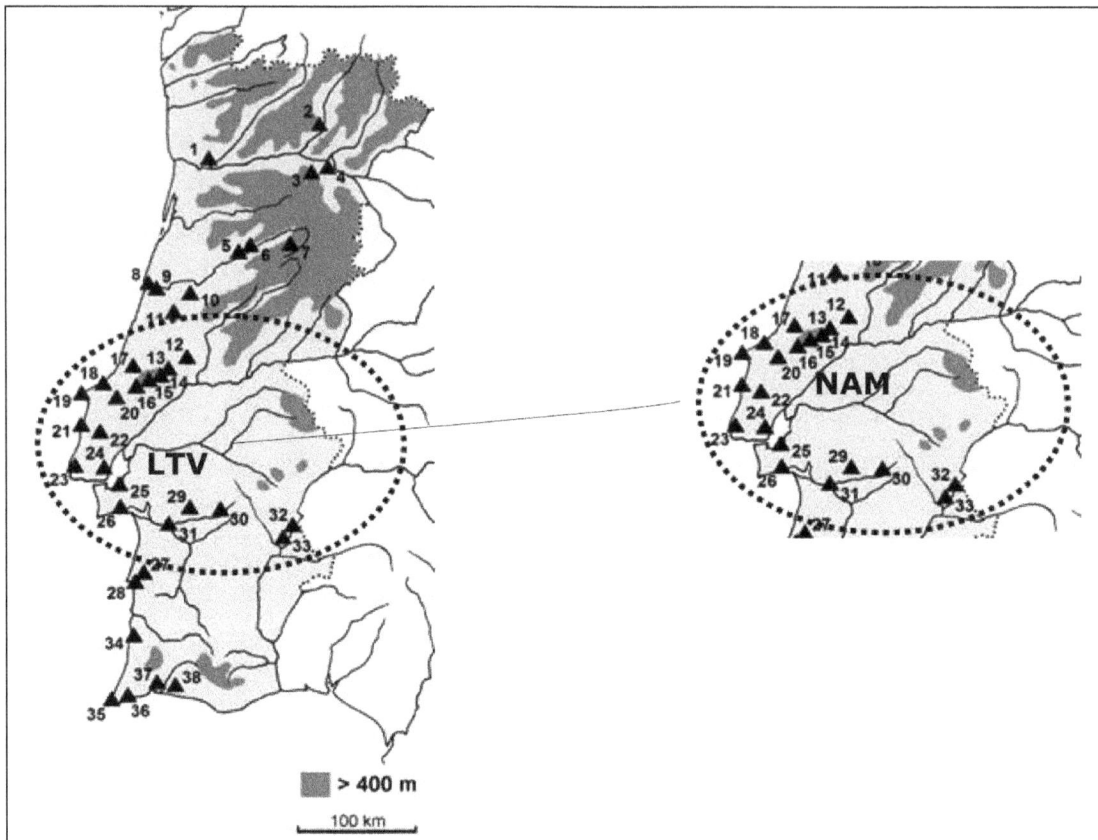

Fig. 6.1. Early Neolithic sites in Portugal: LTV as "no-man´s land"
(based on DINIZ e CARVALHO, in press)

the fluvial channels and of the river bars (Ramos *et al.*, 2001, p. 163; Ramos *et al.*, 2006) are responsible for a changing landscape.

River regime stabilized only in recent times, when in the eighteen century, it was artificial changed, between Valada e Vila Franca de Xira, from several channels to a single one (Azevêdo *et al.*, 2006, p. 65).

Probably the Lower Tagus Valley (LTV) left bank looked like – during maximum transgression in the Middle Holocene (around 6900 cal BP (Freitas *et al.*, 2006) – a salty marsh with some river bars and steeped quaternary terraces suitable for human occupation. In fact, until now, all data about Neolithic settlers came from quaternary terraces where gravel and cobbles river deposits were systemically used as raw material source.

That means that the rich alluvial plain of LTV is a recent (historical?) aspect of the landscape, as the soils great agricultural capability. In Middle Holocene, the region was under estuarine regime with salty waters in Lower Tagus and in final courses of its tributaries.

Therefore, the remarkable and historical fertility of Tagus alluvial plain is a recent feature of the landscape, since salty lands are unsuitable for agricultural practices. On the contrary, hunting, gathering and fishing were, due to

estuarine conditions of Middle Holocene, valuable activities.

In fact, Neolithic settlement and economic patterns would have been deeply constrain by these landscape dynamics with changing conditions from an estuary to an alluvial plain, from a salt to sweet water river, with variably submerged and emerged lands.

These landscape features probably did not attract Neolithic permanent settlement but we know – from recent rescue work and field survey – that LTV left bank is not a "no-mans land" during Middle Holocene like it seems until now. In spite of being irregular, very high fluvial (Ramos *et al.*, 2001) and eolic sedimentation rate cover up paleotopography making field survey a hard task. Archaeological horizons under thick layers of fluvial and eolic sands may never, or only by chance, be found – e.g. from Entre Valas core came from 10.7 m depth organic material dated from 6960 cal PB (Azevedo *et al.*, 2006b, p. 65). This fact could explain why so few data are known from this area – a natural corridor between Estremadura limestone massifs and central Alentejo granitic plains.

Today there are not yet models to explain neolithisation in the area (how, when, and why first agro-pastoralist communities arrived, how they settled, how they use the landscape) but new data from archaeological and

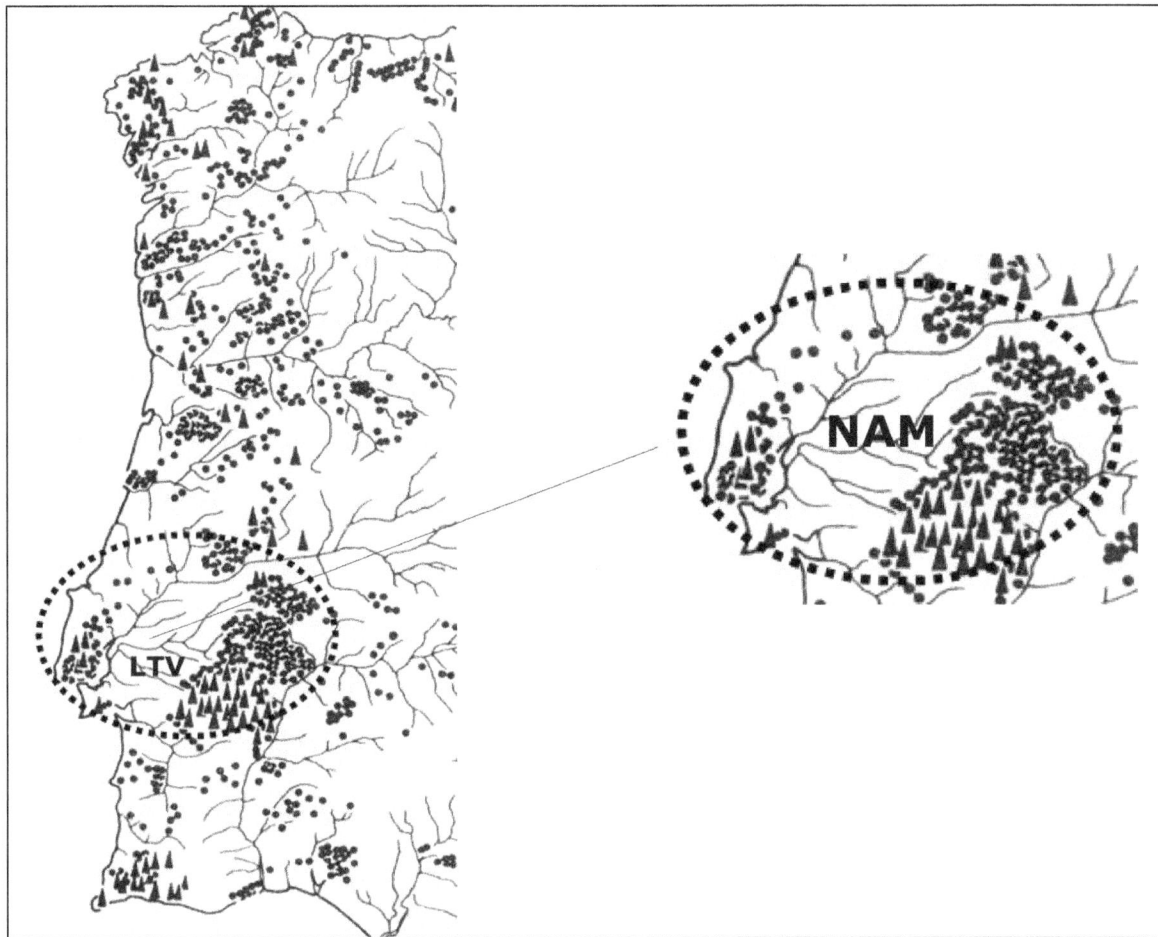

Fig. 6.2. Megalithic monuments in Portugal: no information on LTV (based on KALB, P., 1989)

geomorphological research projects will fill the gap showing that archaeological maps with no Neolithic dots in LTV left bank were a archaeographic, not a historical issue.

OLD PERSPECTIVES

Traditionally, the lower Tagus valley is considered "no-man's land" during neolithisation process.

In fact, in final Mesolithic hunter-gathers occupied intensively this area (between 7500 and 6300 BP). These occupations had no correspondence in later periods. The available data of the neolithisation process in LTV can be summarized on punctual information of ORZ1 (Gonçalves e Daveau, 1983-84) and the few shreds of impressed pottery on the upper levels of Muge shell-middens (Arnaud, 1987).

Looking at archaeological cartography we can observe that Estremadura and central Alentejo have a distinct volume of information.

At Estremadura, on the limestone massifs, the presence of neolithic groups is known since 6400 BP.

Cardial Neolithic caves sites (Gruta do Almonda and Gruta do Caldeirão) revealed an important part of information (Zilhão, 2000). However, the archaeological site Pena d'Água (rock-shelter) presents a large chrono-stratigraphic sequence, where are represented different moments of the neolithisation process. Radiocarbon chronology shows a Cardial Neolithic since 6400 BP, a epi-Cardial Neolithic since 5200 BP and a middle Neolithic since 5000 BP (Carvalho, 1998a).

In Central Alentejo archaeological investigation knew an increase since the 90's of the XX century (Calado, 2001), but just only a few early Neolithic sites have been excavated. Making a comparison with the middle Neolithic, there's a scarce of information. Early Neolithic groups are presented in this region since 6000 BP, as demonstrated by an AMS radiocarbon date on bone, collected in a domestic structure of the open air site Valada do Mato (Diniz, 2001). Middle Neolithic groups are traditionally connected with megalithic monuments, in accordance with Leisner interpretation for Poço da Gateira (Leisner e Leisner, 1951). The monument architecture and the artefactual assemblage (trapezes, non-decorated pottery, and polish instruments) dated this site, based on typological criteria. No radiocarbon chronology is available.

Cal B.C. (2 sigma)

		6500	6000	5500	5000	4500	4000	3500	3000
Lower Tagus Valley (LTV)	Cabeço da Arruda								
	Cabeço da Arruda								
	Cabeço da Arruda								
	Cabeço da Arruda								
	Cabeço da Arruda								
	Mta. Sebastião								
	Mta. Sebastião								
	Mta. Sebastião								
	Mta. Sebastião								
	Mta. Sebastião								
Estremadura (limestone massifs)	Caldeirão								
	Caldeirão								
	Caldeirão								
	Caldeirão								
	Caldeirão								
	Caldeirão								
	Caldeirão								
	Almonda								
	Almonda								
	Pena d'Água								
	Pena d'Água								
	Pena d'Água								
	Pena d'Água								
Central Alentejo	Valada do Mato								

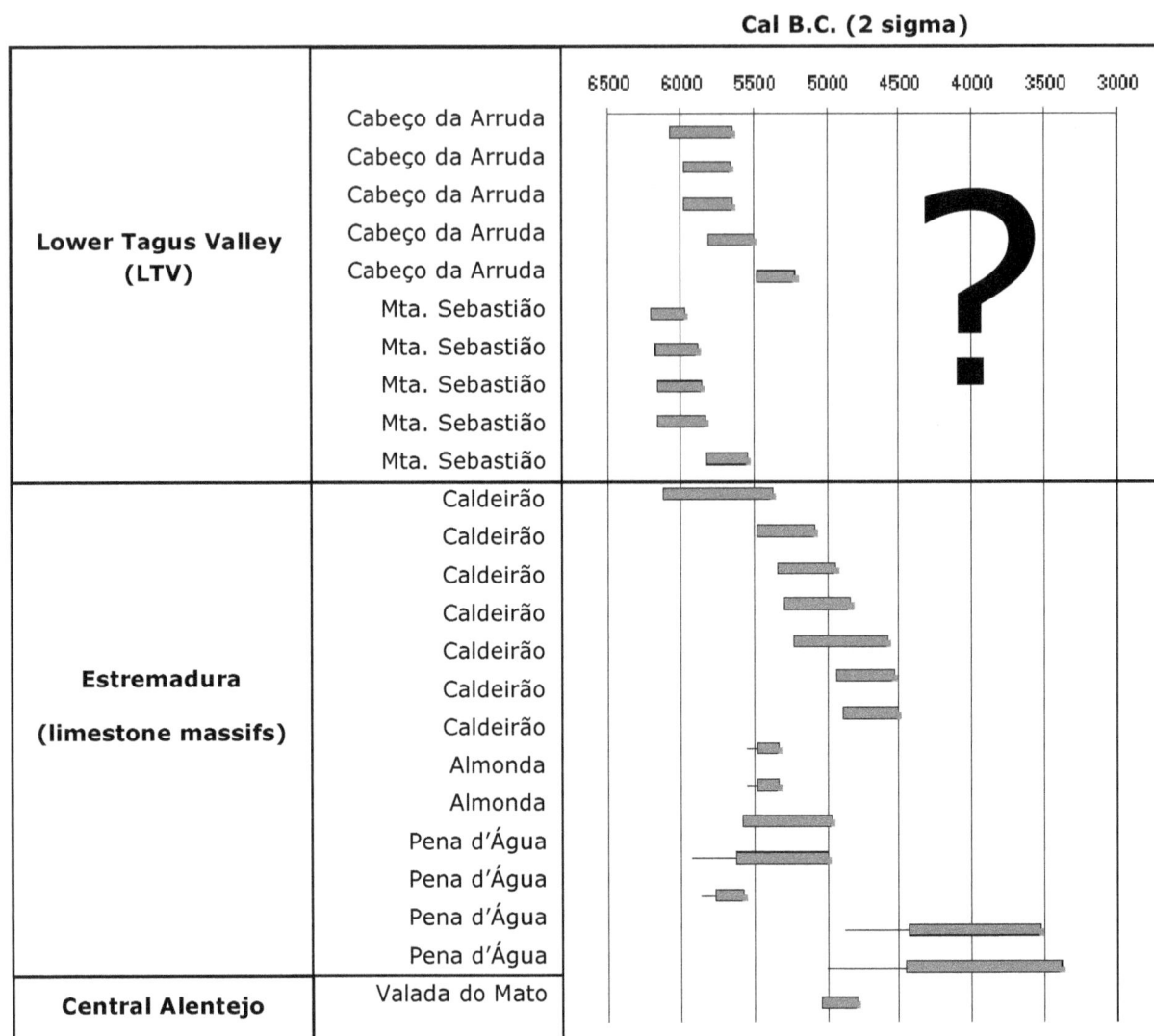

Fig. 6.3. Calibrated radiocarbon chronology of late Mesolithic, early and middle Neolithic sites at LTV, Estremadura and Central Alentejo

NAM Project pretends fill the gap in the archaeological record based on:

1. new available data, that appears during the construction of A13 highway;

2. new archaeological survey.

NEW DATA

The main aim of this chapter is to present four new Neolithic open air sites (Casas Velhas do Coelheiro; Vala Real; Monte da Foz I; Moita do Ourives) revealed by recent works in the area. The archaeological remains from these sites allow us to start thinking about last hunter-gathered societies and first agropastoralist groups in Lower Tagus Valley left bank. These, still preliminary, data are not the result of any systematic research project since it was recovered during surveying projects and rescue excavations.

Casas Velhas do Coelheiro (Salvaterra de Magos)

Casas Velhas do Coelheiro is an open-air site situated in the district of Salvaterra de Magos, placed in quaternary terrace overlying Coelheiro's stream. In fact, the only landscape domain from this archaeological site is Coelheiro's stream.

A local history student identified it. According to surface material observed along an area of 3000 m^2, he defined it as a Neolithic settlement. The only archaeological work carried out at this site was field survey. The material culture coming from the surface reveals a high number of different kinds of artefacts.

The ceramic is highly represented by a fragmental assemblage of decorated and undecorated sherds. Decorated pottery show different types of impressed, incised and plastic motifs. There is an undecorated pottery sherd with only a horizontal incised line below the rim. Typological analysis of the sherds showed that they belonged to spherical vessels with a circular mouth.

The lithics, which used local raw materials, are represented by flint laminary products (bladelets and borers) and by a quartzite production system (macroindustry of flakes and retouched flakes). It is interesting to note, the total absence of polished stone items in surface material.

These data suggest, according to typological criteria, that Casas Velhas do Coelheiro is, probably, a settlement of the late Early Neolithic. The decorated pottery sherds and the laminary products present parallels with artefacts recovered from other well-known settlements in southern Portugal and Estremadura. However, it is very important to remember that this site and the data it provides were not a result of an excavation but of a surveying project.

For the moment, it is impossible to define the subsistence strategy of groups who lived in Casas Velhas do Coelheiro, but its location, near the Coelheiro's stream, and the absence of artefacts connected to agriculture will take us to suggest that the neighbouring resources (aquatic resources) were still very important to those groups.

Vala Real (Salvaterra de Magos)

Located in the district of Salvaterra de Magos, Vala Real is an open air site that was identified and partly excavated by a rescue work that took place during the construction of A13 (Highway Santarém-Algarve). The site is situated in quaternary terrace over a large alluvial plain near Mago's stream, its only landscape domain (Aldeias e Gaspar, 2004). Geologically, sandy deposits characterize Vala Real.

The excavations took place in the area affected by the highway, where archaeological material was not *in situ*. The contexts and the data resulted from this archaeological work are related to post-depositional disturbances and slop movements (Aldeias e Gaspar, 2004). However, the several sedimentary sequences observed by the authors yielded to the archaeological record vestiges of the Neolithic.

The material culture brought out by the excavation showed a very high lithic artefact density and a very low ceramic density. There were only three decorated sherds, one with horizontal incised lines, one with a plastic motif with impressions and another one (the only decorated rim) with a plastic motif. In forty-two sherds, only six had rim. A very fragmented assemblage defines the ceramic, but, according to the authors, it was possible to understand their typological form, simple ones and spherical vessels (Aldeias e Gaspar, 2004).

The lithic economy is represented by local raw material exploitation according to products function. Laminary products, rare in the archaeological record, are flint made and bladelets and a prismatic borer represent them. The

only prove of microlithic industry is represented by a flint crescent. On the other hand, quartzite industry is well represented. Quartzite (and quartz, in a very low density) is associated to flake production, and according to the authors, the site function, placed near by a quartzite source, is related to raw material availability (Aldeias e Gaspar, 2004).

In lithic industry, is also interesting to note the presence of a flint arrowhead. This artefact type is known only in the Neolithic settlements of Portuguese southwest cost.

Despite the innumerable limitations inherent in the study of an archaeological find of this type, according to the authors, Vala Real is an Early Neolithic settlement and this chronological conclusion is compatible with archaeologycal evidence. Once again, the typological criteria was used for chronological and cultural definition, fact related with the absence of eco-facts and the unequivocal parallels in the lithics with Neolithic contexts in the Limestone Massifs of Estremadura (Aldeias e Gaspar, 2004).

According to the authors, the numerous presences of burnt cobbles in archaeological record could suggest the existence of hearths in the settlement. These hearts were dismantled during the erosion of soil covers and land in this area by slop movement (Aldeias e Gaspar, 2004).

Now, the material culture removed from the excavation in Vala Real is the best data available. For the future, it could be possible to make some soundings in the original place of the site, and then we will try to study some issues and questions that are still opened and unsolved.

Monte da Foz I (Benavente)

The site Monte da Foz I is located in Benavente's district. It is an open-air site identified during a surface work and it was partly excavated by a rescue excavation (directed by two of the signatories) that took place during the construction of A10 (Highway Arruda dos Vinhos – Benavente). The site is situated in large plain of a quaternary terrace, near Sorraia River. Geologically, Monte da Foz I is characterized by sandy deposits. The surface material can be observed in a large area of 2 ha (Neves e Rodrigues, 2006).

Excavation took place in different areas affected by the highway. Twenty-two soundings of 2 x 2 m^2 were made and the results were very similar, except in four squares (20m^2). The deposits were excavated by natural stratigraphic units and systematically dry sieved. The layers were highly disturbed by roots and large burrowing animals. The area where Monte da Foz I is placed suffered, in the last century a high level of farming work using heavy machines. The degree of destruction suffered in large areas is visible.

In all the soundings vestiges of Neolithic occupation were recovered. During material culture analysis, it was possible to identify two different moments in Neolithic period: late Early Neolithic and Late Neolithic/ Calcolithic.

In some soundings it was very difficult to understand where it ends one human occupation and starts the other. The sandy deposits, linked to post-depositional disturbances and burrowing could put two occupations in direct stratigraphic contact, making a palimpsest of two different occupations. Only in laboratory, by typological and technological analysis of the material culture it is possible to define a correct and secure chronology, for the stratigraphic sequences. Studying Monte da Foz I data means dealing with several issues related with settlement geographic definition and horizontal stratification (Neves e Rodrigues, 2006).

The four squares above mentioned (20m²), were the only ones where were found a secure and preserved archaeological context. That context showed a high artefact density probably related to late Early Neolithic. The archaeological record is very rich and brought out artefacts of all types and technology. The ceramic is defined by a very large assemblage of undecorated sherds and undecorated sherds with only a horizontal incised line below the rim. The decorated pottery recovered are in lower number when compared with the undecorated or the ones with a horizontal line below the rim. They were decorated with different types of impressed, incised and plastic motifs. In the decorated pottery, the incised sherds are in higher number. The pottery decoration had similarities in other contexts of Early Neolithic in southern Portugal. There is also one sherd of cardial pottery, but its meaning is minor in the archaeological record when compared with the rest of the ceramics. Typological analysis showed that they belonged to spherical vessels with a circular mouth.

In addition to pottery, there are some amphibolites polished stone items (2 fragments of hand axes and two adzes). They are in lower number in the archaeological record but its importance is unquestionable.

As well as the ceramic, the lithics appeared in large number in this context. Flint and quartz laminary products brought out an interesting number of blades, prismatic borers and bladelets. Microliths and geometric armatures are well represented by segments, crescents and trapezes. However, quartzite production system (macroindustry of flakes and borers) is the most represented.

Associated with material culture was a habitat structure. It seems to be a "cuvette" of hardened, darkish sands containing burnt cobbles. This type of structure has parallels in other contexts of Neolithic settlements of Portuguese southwest cost. The scientists who worked in those areas named these structures as hearths. With the purpose of getting any evidence of organic material and eco-fact, sediment sample was saved.

These data suggest a settlement of late Early Neolithic in Monte da Foz I. Even no absolute chronology has been obtained for that context is possible to define it according to typological criteria. On the other hand, it is important to note, that Monte da Foz I had other human occupations which are not well defined, Late Neolithic/Calcolithic. The results that come from these archaeological works have to be carefully study. Some artefacts chronology and cultural definition are not very sharp, especially between two distinct moments in the Portuguese Neolithic (Neves e Rodrigues, 2006).

Site future works will focus in the typological and technology analysis of the artefacts. Future fieldwork will wait for the results of the laboratory.

Moita do Ourives (Companhia das Lezírias, Benavente)

The archaeological site Moita do Ourives was identified during the construction of the A13 (Highway Santarém-Algarve). The area affected for the construction of the road was integrally excavated (directed by one of the signatories), in a total of about 150m². The site is located in the geographic area of Benavente's district and is located inside the area of the Companhia das Lezírias S.A. It is an open-air site near to the St. Estevão's stream, not having any domain of the landscape or defensive concern. Geologically, sandy deposits characterize Moita do Ourives. The excavation took place in a large open area allowing the identification of preserved archaeological contexts, in a stratigraphic sequence of 50 cm. Deposits were excavated by natural stratigraphic units and systematically dry sieved (Rodrigues, 2007).

Recent farming works or post-depositional disturbances did not affect the archaeological record. On the other hand, roots or animal burrows originate the only disturbances, which made some vertical dispersion of the archaeological artefacts.

The main archaeological context brought out by this work was the three hearths recovered in distinct areas of the settlement. An assemblage of cracked burnt cobbles makes these structures. However, there were not, associated with the hearths, eco-facts, fauna remains or any other evidence of organic material. Therefore, a sample of sediment was saved from each habitat structure.

The material culture in the archaeological record is in a significant number. The ceramics are characterized for being undecorated, only existing two body sherds with incised motifs. The forms correspond, typologically, to goblets and simple sphericals. Polished stone items are represented with only one artefact, an amphibolite's hand axe.

Lithics are in majority in the archaeological record. Bladelets and a single blade represented flint laminary products. The microindustry and geometric production is represented a by flint trapeze. However, quartzite lithic

Fig. 6.4. Rescue work at Moita do Ourives

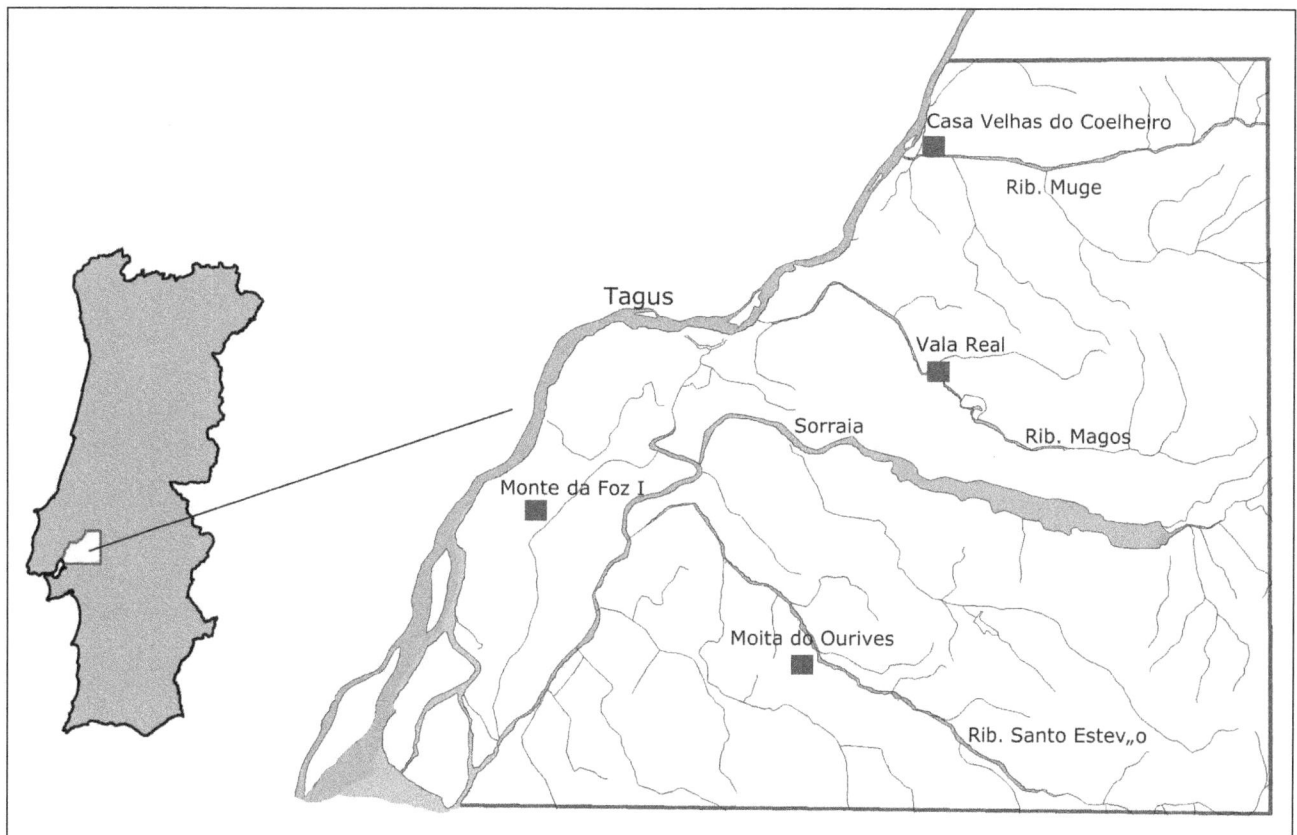

Fig. 6.5. Geographic distribution of archaeological sites in LTV (new data)

production system (macroindustry of flakes and borers) is highly represented in archaeological record.

From the study of the material culture and looking to similar contexts in Central Alentejo (Megalithic monuments) and Estremadura (Limestone Massifs of Estremadura; Pena d' Água), these data suggest that Moita do Ourives was a Middle Neolithic settlement. The artefact density and its homogeneity put the range of occupation for this site in a short period during the Middle Neolithic (Rodrigues, 2007).

The absence of eco-facts in the archaeological record does not help to characterize group subsistence strategies, which remain future research central goal.

OLD PERSPECTIVES AND NEW DATA

In sum, the data now available show us an important group of archaeological sites for understanding Neolithisation process in Lower Tagus Valley left bank. First, they allow us to talk about an effective Early and Middle Neolithic settlement in this area in opposition to the old and traditional view of the "no-man's land" that took place after the abandonment of the Muge shell middens around 6300 BP.

From these data, we can say that Lower Tagus Valley left bank was occupied, attending to typological criteria, if not earlier, by the end of the 6th millennium BC/ first half of the 5[th.] Small Early Neolithic groups are settled in quaternary terraces, near water streams, exploring local available raw materials (cobbles, quartz and rare flint from gravel deposits), with decorated poterry and rare, or none, polished stone tools. Due to large containers and agricultural tools absence economic strategies, attending to local landscape features, must have remained largely of a broad spectrum type in temporary habitats.

By the Middle Neolithic, some changes occurred. Poterry became undecorated, some polished artefacts appear and flint from primary sources was used. Although so, data from Moita do Ourives (with no large poterry containers, perishable structures and only a single polished stone tool) do not fit with an agricultural group material record.

If some kind of environmental adjustment could have been made, during Early and Middle Neolithic, giving raise to settlements patterns deeply related to LTV landscape features is a unsolved question that only future field and laboratory work can answer.

On the other hand, these new archaeological data are associated with several problems/questions/issues:

– Settlements partially excavated and only in small and restricted areas

– Archaeological record showing sites with large and different chronological and cultural human occupations

– Sandy deposits bringing taphonomic problems which are linked eco-facts absence in archaeological record

– Sites chronological definitions have been made using only typological criteria.

These new data and the questions above mentioned are the stimulus of the multidisciplinary research project NAM, focus on 6th and 5th millennia cal B.C time span.

In future phases, we have the purpose of changing these issues into scientific realities. New research strategies will bring new data that will be used to discuss settlement patterns, economic strategies and cultural affiliation of these Early and Middle Neolithic groups, in a changing landscape.

Therefore, future research trends will focus on:

– geomorphological data – Lower Tagus Holocene evolution;

– field survey – spacial analysis and settlement patterns;

– excavation work – habitat structures/habitat function/

– artefacts and eco-facts – relative and absolute chronology/economic strategies/ cultural affiliations;

that will allow us to study and "rebuild" the way of life of the last hunter-gathered societies and first agropastoralist groups.

References

ALDEIAS, V., GASPAR, R. (2005) – O sítio da Vala Real (Salvaterra de Magos). Contributo para o conhecimento do Neolítico antigo no Baixo Tejo. Actas do IV Congresso de Arqueologia Peninsular, no prelo.

ARNAUD, J. MORAIS (1987) – Os concheiros mesolíticos dos vales do Tejo e Sado: semelhanças e dissemelhanças. *Arqueologia*. Porto. 15, p. 53-64.

AZEVÊDO, T., RAMOS. C., PEREIRA, A.R., NUNES, E., FREITAS, C., ANDRADE, C., PEREIRA, D. (2006a) – The Geotarif Project. *Tagus Floods '06 Workshop*. Lisboa, p. 11- 14

AZEVÊDO, T., NUNES, E., RAMOS. C., PEREIRA, A.R., FREITAS, C., ANDRADE, C., PEREIRA, D. (2006b) – The Tagus River and its Historical Floods (Santarém, Portugal). *Tagus Floods '06 Workshop*. Lisboa, p. 64-67

BENITO, G. (2006) – Paleoflood and Historical Flood Records along the Middle Tagus River Catchment: Climatic and Flood Hazard Implications. *Tagus Floods '06 Workshop*. Lisboa, p.35

CABRAL, J. (2006) – Active Tectonic Structures in the Lower Tagus Valley: the Sate of the Art. *Tagus Floods '06 Workshop*. Lisboa, p.53-55

CARVALHO, A.F. (1998a) – Abrigo da Pena d' Água (Rexaldia, Torres Novas): resultados das campanhas de sondagem (1992-1997). *Revista Portuguesa de Arqueologia*. Lisboa. 1:2. pp. 39-72

CALADO, M. (2001) – Da Serra d'Ossa ao Guadiana. Um estudo de pré-história regional. *Trabalhos de Arqueologia 19*, Instituto Português de Arqueologia, Lisboa.

DINIZ, M., CARVALHO, A.F. (in press) – Le Néolithiquen ancient au Portugal: aprés 35 annés. BSPHF.

FREITAS, C., ANDRADE, C., AZEVÊDO, T., PEREIRA, A.R., RAMOS, C., NUNES, E., PEREIRA, D. (2006) – Understanding Lateglacial and Holocene Environmental changes Trough the Sedimentological Study of a Core (Santarém Region). *Tagus Floods '06 Workshop*. Lisboa, p.85-89

GONÇALVES, V.S. e DAVEAU, S. (1983-84) – Programa para o estudo da antropização do Baixo Tejo e afluentes: Projecto para o estudo da antropização do Vale do Sorraia (ANSOR). *Clio/Arqueologia, Revista da Uniarch*, vol.1, Lisboa, p. 203-206.

LEISNER, G. e LEISNER, V. (1951) – *Antas do Concelho de Reguengos de Monsaraz. Materiais para o estudo da cultura megalítica em Portugal*, Lisboa, Instituto para a Alta Cultura.

NEVES, C., RODRIGUES, A.F. (2006) – *Monte da Foz I*. Relatório Final dos trabalhos arqueológicos. Policopiado

RAMOS, C., REIS, E., PEREIRA, A.R., AZEVEDO, T., NUNES, E., FREITAS, M.C., ANDRADE, C. (2001) – Late Holocene Evolution of the Lower Tagus Alluvial Plain and Heavy Metals Content: Preliminary Results. *Cuadernos de Investigación Geográfica*. Universidad de La Rioja, 27, p. 163-178.

RODRIGUES, A.F. (2005) – Moita do Ourives: o Neolítico médio na Bacia do Baixo Tejo, Actas do IV Congresso de Arqueologia Peninsular, no prelo.

PEREIRA, A., RAMOS, C., AZEVÊDO, T., NUNES, E., FREITAS, C., ANDRADE, C., PEREIRA, D. (2006) – Geomorphological Assesment of the Middle Tagus Alluvial Plain. *Tagus Floods '06 Workshop*. Lisboa, p.79 – 81

ZILHÃO, J. (2000) – From the Mesolithic to the Neolithic in the Iberian Peninsula. *Europe's First Farmers*, ed. T. Douglas Price, Cambridge, Cambridge University Press, p. 144-182.

EARLY NEOLITHIC AT THE SERPIS VALLEY, ALICANTE, SPAIN

J. BERNABEU AUBÁN, LL. MOLINA BALAGUER, T. OROZCO KÖHLER,
A. DIEZ CASTILLO

Departament de Prehistòria i Arqueologia. Universitat de Valencia

C.M. BARTON

Department of Anthropology. Arizona State University

Summary: *After two decades of continued field work developing survey and excavation projects, the Serpis valley represent a privileged area for analysing the origin and evolution of the first agricultural societies in the Iberian peninsula.*
The information generated in all fields enlights the discussion about the Neolithic; furthermore it allows a social characterization of the cardial groups different from the traditional one in the peninsula.
Key-Words: *Neolithisation process; Serpis Valley; Cardial groups; Social organization*

Resumo: *O vale do Serpis é hoje, depois de duas décadas de trabalhos de terreno, que incluíram prospecções e escavações, uma área privilegiada para analisar a origem e evolução das primeiras sociedades agrícolas na Península Ibérica.*
A informação gerada nas diferentes vertentes destes projectos permite esclarecer distintos aspectos acerca do Neolítico e caracterizar os grupos cardiais, num quadro social distinto do tradicionalmente admitido.
Palavras-chave: *Processo de Neolitização; vale do Serpis; Grupos cardiais; Organização social*

THE SERPIS VALLEY

These geographical area comprises an extensive territory of irregular topography: it corresponds to an inland hillside region crossed by a series of valleys of different flow and banking. This relief is located in the external side of the Betic Ranges, in an ENE-WSW axis that determines the orientation of the main fluvial artery: the Serpis river (or riu d'Alcoi). A set of small fluvial streams converge into its middle and upper basins (fig. 7.1), which usually take the name of the small valleys they cut (Penàguila, Barxell-Polop, Agres, Alcalà, Ceta, etc.).

The diversity of ecological niches within this region has favoured human presence in Late Prehistory. Thus, archaeological investigations, beginning at the end of 19th century, have highlighted an important number of human deposits dated within the Holocene (Bernabeu *et al*, in press)

As regards the Neolithic, the contributions of La Sarsa (San Valero, 1950) and, above all, l'Or (Martí Oliver, 1977; Martí Oliver *et al*., 1980), as well as other caves located in nearby fields such as Cendres (Bernabeu *et al*. 1999a), evidenced a paradox that explain some part of the discussion about peninsular Neolithic until now. Thus, if on one hand these sites clearly show the presence of a society with full use of domestic resources, on the other, this situation did not match the generalized absence of village spaces typical of definite Neolithic groups.

The development of a continued field-work on these area between the last two decades (1986-2006), both surveys and excavations, allows us to offer an image very different from the empirical record corresponding to the first farmers (Bernabeu *et al*., in press).

Summing up, we currently posses a documental *corpus* (fig. 7.2) that is not only extensive but also extremely solid that derives in the possibility to offer a rather precise chronological frame to start posing hypotheses about the socio-economic dynamics generated by these societies.

THE MESOLITHIC GAP AND THE NEOLITHIC ORIGINS

Stratified assemblages coming from different excavations at Serpis Valley and the neighborhood areas have allowed one of us to propose an archaeological sequence on the basis of ceramic evolution criteria (Bernabeu, 1989).

The oldest phases – Neolithic IA – show an iconographic and formal repertoire related to the cultural tradition of the impressed-ware ceramics in the Mediterranean. Cardial decoration, supposes an important decorative technique; subsequent phases (NIB and NIC) are defined on the variability of decorative tecniques. Usualy, Neolithic IB, with incised and impressed pottery, is knewed as Epicardial.

Preceramic industries are knewed as Geometric Mesolithic. Stratigraphic assemblages in all the iberian peninsula show an archaeological sequence based on the shape of geometric tools: Phase A, with trapeziums; and Phase B, with triangles.

Available radiocarbon chronology, based on the dating of samples from singular events to avoid taphonomic problems and the "old wood effect", offers a picture of population continuity between c. 6500 and 2200 cal. BC that is truncated in two occasions (fig. 7.3):

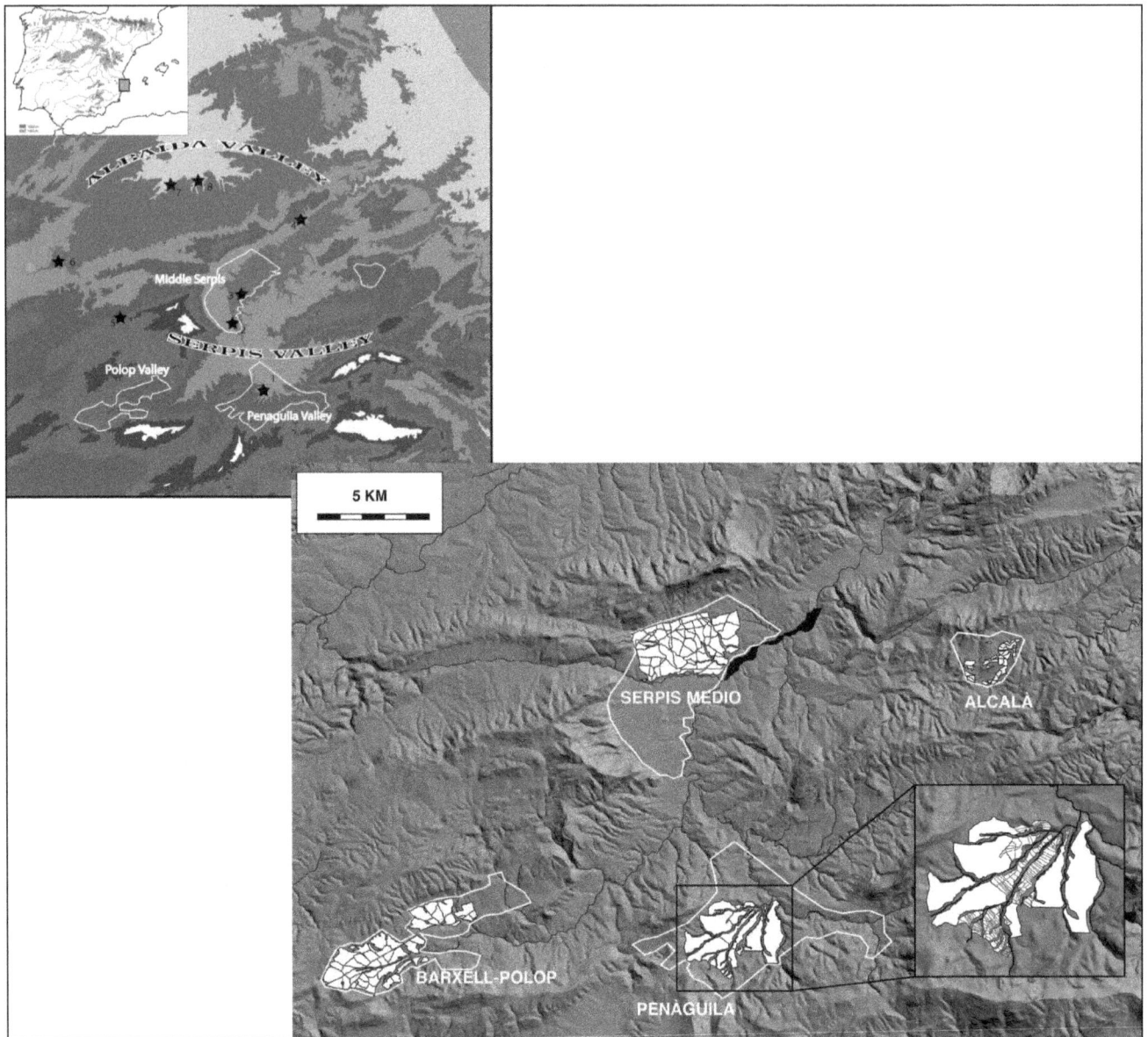

Fig. 7.1. Map of the Serpis valley, showing some of the most knewed Neolithic sites (left),
and the units used in the survey projects

a. Between c. 6100-5600/5500 BC, corresponding to a later phase of the Geometric Mesolithic. This moment would indicate a real hiatus between the Mesolithic and Neolithic.

b. Between c. 4200-3900 BC, corresponding to the Neolithic IIA-IIB transition in the regional sequence. For the time being, we are not in a position to suppose that this hiatus corresponds to a real interruption in the habitation of the valley.

In the study area, diverse deposits have been excavated with levels belonging to the Mesolithic (Bernabeu et al., in press). In all the cases, the documented industries belong to the initial phase of the mesolithic (A stage). The dates available agree with the well-known ones for the Iberian Peninsula (c. 6500-6000 lime BC.). In spite of the

efforts made, we do not have in the Serpis valley any layer nor date that can be paralleled with the B stage.

We were, therefore in a situation of rupture in the mesolthic/neolthic transition, of way similar to which it happens in other parts of the Mediterranean (Biagi, 2003; Runnels, 2003). This constitutes a endorsement to the hypothesis of demic diffusion when saying that the new neolithic groups would tend to settle on regions with null or very little mesolithic presence.

Nevertheless, this an aspect of the problem. Since the groups of the Mesolithic before occupied this territory until centuries, our problem consists of trying to give explanation to the leading ones of this process. In our opinion two routes of interpretation could be logically possible, although with unequal empirical support.

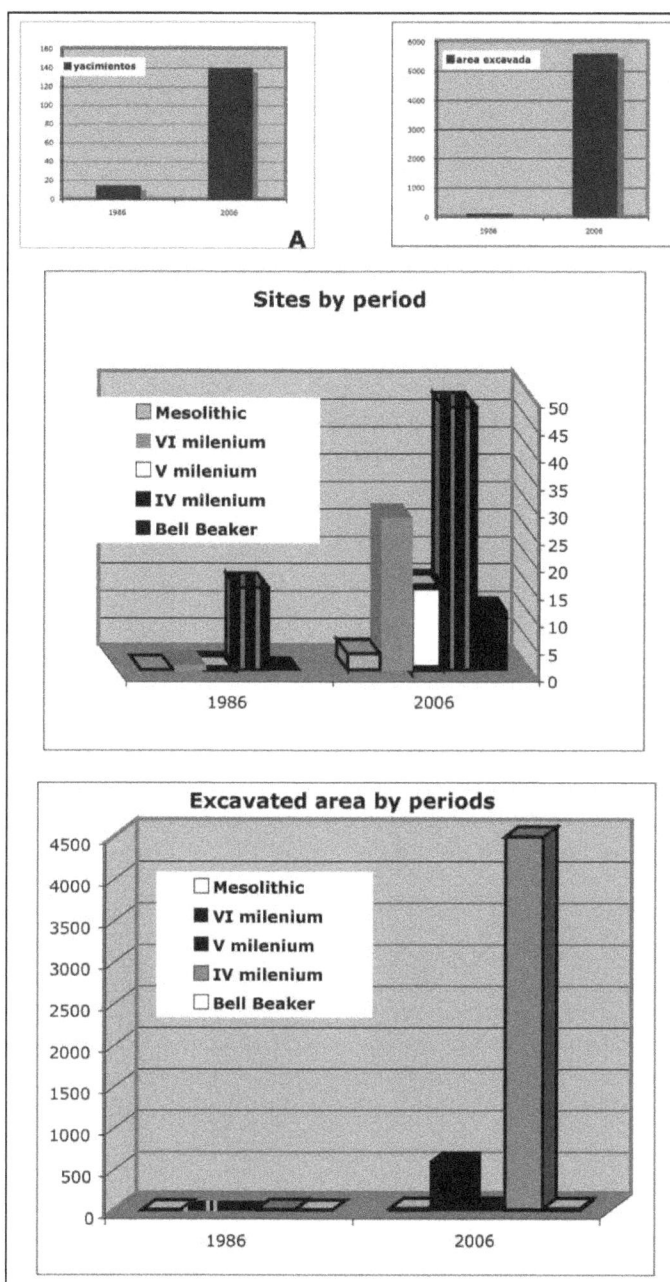

Fig. 7.2. The effect of the continued fieldwork in the archaeological record, taking the dates of 1986 and 2006 as representatives of the current situation before and after the fieldwork. A) Total number of sites; B) Total excavated surface; C) Number of sites by periods; D) excavated area by periods

a. The situation described reflects the reality and, consequently, the causes of the abandonment of this region must look for within the mesolithic groups. There are little where to look for.

Certain indications, as the study of the coastline made as opposed to Cendres cave (Fumanal, 2001) seems to indicate that after a phase of stability c. 7500BP, took place an abrupt increase of the marine level in this zone. This date close to of the available ones for the set of the mesolthic sites and, consequently, could to be maintain the chronological compatibility between both

b. Some imbalance in the information exists so that, either the end of the Mesolithic phase A is more recent, or the beginning of the Neolithic is much older, or both things simultaneously.

The impact of the neolitización might explain easier the rapid disappearance of the mesolithic groups. The assimilation and/or the migration to neighboring groups would be glimpsed as the mechanisms capable of explaining this process. Nevertheless, this hypothesis does not have empirical support. The available dates for the beginnings of the Neolithic in the Western Mediterranean difficultly can exceed 5700 cal BC; whereas we

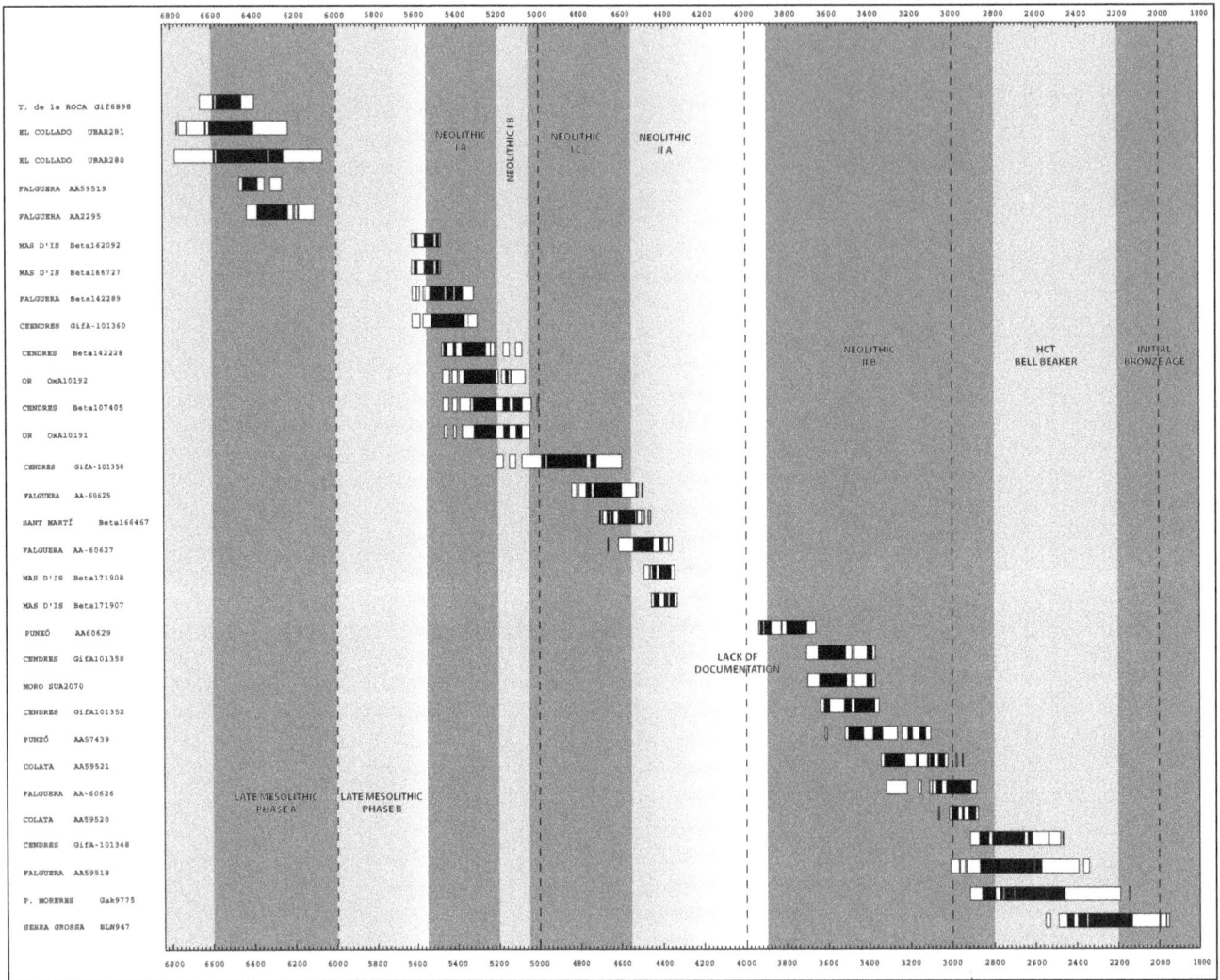

Fig. 7.3. Radiocarbon dates showing the evolution from the Late Mesotithic to the begining of Bronze Age.
Based on short-live samples of singular events

do not know dates that locate the phase A of the Mesolíthic beyond c. 6000 cal. BC.

The latter point sends us to the question of the initial chronology of the neolithic, where diverse aspects of taphonomic character impede its comprehension. The direct available dates (based on domestic species) for the Iberian Peninsula show a gradation and a speed of expansion compatible with the forecasts of the maritime pioner model. Besides, the comparison between the series proceeding from the cardial and epicardial contexts, associated with domesticaton, show that the first ones are earlier (Bernabeu, 2006b).

In agreement with the maritime pioner model, it was of waiting, simultaneously, for a low demographic initial level and the conformation of what it is named "foundational enclaves" whose impact on the mesolithic groups might have a revitalizing effect (the forunder effect), causing the expansion of the new system. The case of Serpis Valles allows us to present a first image of what could to be one of these enclaves.

THE MAS D'IS AND THE CARDIAL GROUP OF THE SERPIS VALLEY

The discovery and excavation of Mas d'Is Neolithic site (Penàguila, Alicante), combined with the information generated in the basin of the Serpis, has supposed an important change in the consideration of the first farmers (Bernabeu et al., 2003 y 2005).

In effect, the Mas d'Is is slightly more than an early Neolithic village, while close to diverse structures that define the domestic space, there has located an enclosure of big dimensions, dated in the VI millenium cal BC (fig. 7.4).

The area where it is located fit to a former glacis, in which diverse erosive processes took place, giving to a series of deep ravines that cut the platform of miocene marls, at the time that they have dismantled some prehistoric structures. The agricultural transformations have given place to a destruction of the most superficial record, masking of the former topography.

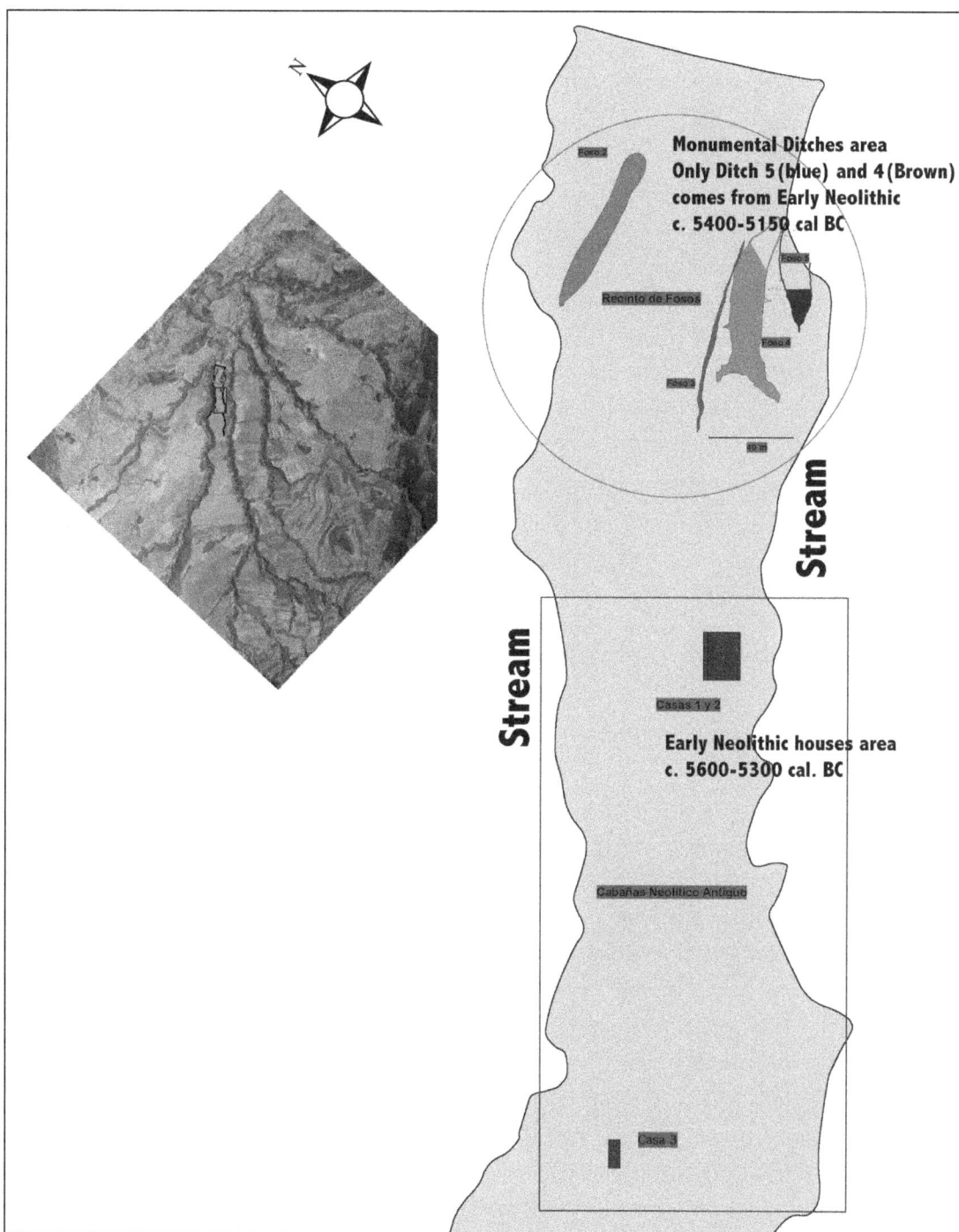

Fig. 7.4. The Mas d'Is site. Left, aerial of the Penàguila valley with the location of the site. Rigth, map of the site showing the location of neolithic houses and the monumental ditches area

Diverse structures are organized around some spaces defined as houses. For what we know, all of them are of rectangular plant with an absidal ending. His external perimeter is defined by posts, with walls of mud (Bernabeu *et al.* 2003). Radiocarbon dates locate these houses between c. 5600-5300 cal. BC.

Towards E., separated from domestic structures, we find a group of monumental ditches defining an en-closure constructed irregularly along a millenium. Of this one,

the part that safely was constructed and used during the Early Neolithic corresponds with the space defined by the Ditches 5 and 4. Both delimit a space that, unfortunately, has been eroded mostly by the adjacent ravine.

In both cases, they are segmented ditches in U section, 12-18m wide and 3,8-4,2m deep. They limit a singular space, in an indefinite way, though their trails present a circular tendency (Orozco *et al.*, in press).

The construction of this enclosure represents the first modification of the landscape to great scale in the Iberian prehistory. Between both, they suppose an investment of work that could overcame 100.000 hours/person.

The singularity of the enclosure built there may be evaluated by many factors (large dimensions, no relation with habitation space). We find it necessary, however, to frame the analysis in the set of features that, along these valleys, make a singular stage that justifies speaking of a strong territorial feature in the first agrarian communities or, at least, of a clear need to fix the boundaries of a territory (Fig. 7.4):

The presence of some caves (Or, Sarsa) with an unusual volume of singular items (Bernabeu *et al.*, 2003, 2006): pottery vessels with symbolic styles, musical instruments, slate bracelets, ochre powder and rock, prepared for mixing colorant stuff, and a strong consumption of sub-adult ovicaprids; there are also small funerary caves in adjacent hills, making true necropolis areas (Bernabeu *et al.* 2001).

This panorama is completed with the location of Macro Schematic rock art sanctuaries, places of important symbolism that are lined up in the borders of the Serpis valleys, with chronologies defined by the superposition of representations, as well as by their pottery parallels (Cardito, 1998; Martí and Hernández, 1988).

All these locations manifest the higher investment on aspects of greater visibility that, in this case, represents a higher symbolic character, indicating the possession and transformation of the space by these social groups. It can be read as a strong process of territorialization and rooting in this space.

We clearly see that labour is directed to ideological aspects –which reinforce intra-group cohesion as well as individual authority. It helps to propose that the social nets mobilizing, organizing and coordinating labour investment in these Neolithic groups in the Serpis valleys also feed on ideological basis (Bernabeu *et al.* 2006a).

Thus, it is the control over the ritual or the ideology what legitimizes certain individuals to mobilize resources on behalf of the group. Ideology has both a symbolic and material component, and constitutes a media to transmit many messages and information; it can materialize in the form of ceremonies, symbolic objects or monuments, reaching the status of an effective source of social power (Earle, 1997). Such materialization makes it possible to spread a doctrine or ideological body among a local group, as well as to establish communication between the power of a central authority and the lot of the people (De Marrais *et al.* 1996). Ideological power may lead to set up and maintain domination relations.

In non-state groups, powerful individuals invariably represent an association: a household, an extended family,

a lineage, a genealogical clan, a village, a tribe (Mann, 1986). Power is held on behalf of the group and it implies neither coercive capacity nor the possibility to get hold of the resources. This kind of societies may present centralized or decentralised ways of power to a higher or lower degree, based –maybe- in the diversity of the sources of social power. Inside them, tensions are expressed, either by the resistance to excessive concentration, or due to the difficulty to impose the will of some over the rest that, in any case, would facilitate the rise and dismantle cycles of the social nets of power.

We can understand the development of power in the first agrarian communities in the Serpis in this sense. Landscape monumentalization in such terms facilitates discussing the development of a collective power resting on the control of the ritual and the ideological mechanisms that allow certain individuals –on behalf of the group- to increasingly mobilize resources. A diachronic reading of the monumental enclosure in Mas d'Is with its documented phases (building, enlarging, abandonment...) indicates that it is a discontinued process prolonged in time that may be understood as the result of the cyclic movements of advance and receding of power structures;

Alternative, it would be possible to construct an equally reasonable explanation of these changes departing from the long-term effects on the landscape of the agriculture and husbandry. The cycle of felling, burning, culturing, shepherding, erosion of the soil, would force the residential change of the groups, in search of the lands not submitted yet to the erosive processes. The effect might be similar to that of the described cycles of power up and down with its corollaries: population concentration and dispersion.

Testing such hypotheses about the complex, recursive dynamics between co-evolving economic, social, and environmental systems will require more than simply acquiring more archaeological data, however. Simulation environments, such as the one we are developing in the MEDLAND project, will allow us to propose and evaluate such hypotheses about the impacts of the changing agricultural cycle on the dispersal or aggregation of population, the growth and collapse of socio-political power.

Finally, it is possible, though slightly probable, that the cardial groups of the Serpis are an exception. The development of the first Neolithic should have produced comparable situations in other peninsular regions and times. We are sure that the continuity in the development of the fieldworks at the moment in course in other regions will produce comparable results with those the described here.

Bibliography

BARTON, C.M., BERNABEU, J., AURA, J.E., GARCÍA, O. 1999: Land-use dynamics and socio-economic change: an example from the Polop Alto valley. *American Antiquity*, 64 (4): 609-634.

BARTON, C.M., BERNABEU, J., AURA, J.E., GARCÍA, O., LA ROCA, N. 2002: Dynamics landscapes, artifact taphonomy and landuse modeling in the Western Mediterranean. *Geoarchaeology*, 17 (2): 155-190.

BARTON, C.M., BERNABEU, J., AURA, J.E., MOLINA, Ll., SCHMICH, S., 2004a: Historical contingency, nonlinearity, and neolithization of the Western Mediterranean. In L. Wandsnider, E. Athanassopoulos (eds.): *Current Issues in Mediterranean Landscape Archaeology*: 99-124. University of Pennsylvania Press. Philadelphia.

BARTON, C.M., BERNABEU, J., AURA, J.E., GARCÍA, O., SCHMICH, S., MOLINA, Ll. 2004b: Long-Term Socioecology and Contingent Landscapes. *Journal of Archaeological Method and Theory*, 11 (3): 253-295.

BARTON, C.M., OROZCO KÖHLER, T. 2001: La Albufera de Gaianes: AC-69 (Gaianes). In *Actuaciones Arqueológicas en la provincia de Alicante*. CD-ROM. Sección de Arqueología del Ilustre Colegio Oficial de Doctores y Licenciados de Alicante.

BERNABEU, J., GUITART, I., PASCUAL, J., Ll., 1989: Reflexiones en torno al patrón de asentamiento en el País Valenciano entre el Neolítico y la Edad del Bronce. *Saguntum-PLAV, 22*: 99-124

BERNABEU, J., PÉREZ RIPOLL, M., MARTÍNEZ VALLE, R. 1999a: Huesos, Neolitización y Contextos Arqueológicos Aparentes. In J. Bernabeu and T. Orozco (eds.): *II Congrés del Neolític a la Península Ibérica. Saguntum-PLAV, extra-2*: 589-596.

BERNABEU, J., BARTON, C.M., GARCÍA PUCHOL, O. LA ROCA, N. 1999b: Prospecciones sistemáticas en el valle del Alcoi (Alicante, España). Primeros resultados. *Arqueología Espacial*, 21: 29-64.

BERNABEU, J., OROZCO KÖHLER, T. 2005: Mas d'Is (Penàguila, Alicante): un recinto monumental del VI milenio cal BC. *III Congreso del Neolítico en la Península Ibérica. 2003, Santander*. Universidad de Cantabria: 485-495.

BERNABEU, J., OROZCO KÖHLER, T., DIEZ CASTILLO, A., GÓMEZ PUCHE, M., MOLINA HERNÁNDEZ, F.J. 2003: Mas d'Is (Penàguila, Alicante): Aldeas y recintos monumentales del Neolítico Inicial en el valle del Serpis. *Trabajos de Prehistoria*, 60, 2: 39-59.

BERNABEU, J., MOLINA, Ll., DIEZ CASTILLO, A., OROZCO KÖHLER, T. 2006: Inequalities and power.

Three millenia of Prehistory in Mediterranean Spain (5600-2000 cal. BC). In Diaz-del-Río and García Sanjuan (eds.) *Social Inequality in Iberian Late Prehistory*. British Archaeological Report, IS, 1525: 97-116.

FAIRÉN JIMÉNEZ, S. 2006: El Paisaje de la Neolitización. Arte Rupestre, poblamiento y mundo funerario en las comarcas centro-meridionales valencianas. Universidad de Alicante. Alicante.

GARCÍA ATIENZAR, G. 2006: Valles, Cuevas y Abrigos. El paisaje pastoril durante el Neolítico de las comarcas centromeridionales del País Valenciano. In I. Grau Mira (ed.): *La aplicación de los SIG en la Arqueología del Paisaje*. Universidad de Alicante. Alicante: 149-170.

GARCÍA PUCHOL, O., AURA J.E. (coords.), 2006: El Abric de la Falguera (Alcoi, Alacant). 8000 años de ocupación humana en la cabecera del Rio de Alcoi. MARQ-CAM-Ajuntament d'Alcoi.

HERNÁNDEZ PÉREZ, M.S. 2005: Del Alto Segura al Turia. Arte Rupestre Pospaleolítico en el arco Mediterráneo. In Hernández and Soler (eds.): *Actas del Congreso de Arte Rupestre en la España Mediterránea (Alicante, 2004)*. Alicante: 45-70.

HERNÁNDEZ PÉREZ, M.S., FERRER MARSET, P., CATALÀ FERRER, E. 1988: *Arte Rupestre en Alicante*. Fundación Banco Exterior. Madrid.

HERNÁNDEZ PÉREZ, M.S.; MARTÍ OLIVER, B. 2000-2001: El Arte Rupestre de la fachada mediterránea: entre la tradición epipaleolítica y la expansión neolítica. *Zephyrus*, 53-54: 241-265.

MARTÍ OLIVER, B. 1977: *Cova de l'Or (Beniarrés, Alicante). Vol. I*. Trabajos Varios del SIP, 51. Valencia.

MARTÍ OLIVER, B., PASCUAL, V., GALLART, M.D., LÓPEZ, P., PÉREZ, M., ACUÑA, J.D., ROBLES, F. 1980: *Cova de l'Or (Beniarrés, Alicante). Vol. II*. Trabajos Varios del SIP, 65. Valencia.

OROZCO KÖHLER, T., BERNABEU, J., MOLINA, Ll. In press: Neolithic enclosures as Power Expression in Mediterranean Spain. In Shaw-Evangelista, L. and Valera, A.C. (coords.) *The Idea of Enclosure in Iberian Prehistory*. XV Congreso UISPP, Lisbon 2006.

SAN VALERO, J. 1950: *La Cueva de La Sarsa (Bocairente, Valencia)*. Trabajos Varios del SIP, 12. Valencia.

TORREGROSA, P., GALIANA, M.F. 2001: El Arte Esquemático del Levante Peninsular: una aproximación a su dimensión temporal. *Millars*, XIV: 153-198.

SOURCES OF MONUMENTALITY: STANDING STONES IN CONTEXT (FONTAÍNHAS, ALENTEJO CENTRAL, PORTUGAL)

Manuel CALADO; Leonor ROCHA

Abstract: The recent excavation at the Fontaínhas megalithic enclosure has allowed us, once again, to confirm the ancient chronologies of this type of monument in the context of the broader regional megalithic sequence.
Actually, the discovery of Early Neolithic-type pottery and lithic artefacts is generally in accordance with the data obtained, in the last years, on several other sites in the South of Portugal.
The regional character of the Alentejan megalithic enclosures, together with their chronological background, forces us to relate them with the specific pattern of the neolithisation of Central Alentejo.
In this context, we re-evaluate the presumed protagonism of the last hunter-gatherers of the Tejo-Sado shell-middens, whose social and cultural complexity, together with their demographic potential, allow us to understand the extraordinary investment implied in the building of these first monuments.
Key-words: Megalithic enclosures; Chronologies; Neolithisation process

Resumo: A recente escavação do recinto megalítico das Fontaínhas permitiu-nos, masi uma vez, confirmar a antiguidade da cronologia deste tipo de monumentos no contexto alargado da sequência megalítica regional.
No recinto das Fontaínhas, a identificação de cerâmicas e de materiais líticos tipologicamente enquadráveis no Neolítico antigo, confirma o quadro geral que tem vindo a ser definido em outros sítios do Sul de Portugal.
O carácter regional dos recintos megalíticos alentejanos, e o seu enquadramento cronológico, leva-nos a relacionar estes monumentos com os padrões específicos da neolitização do Alentejo Central.
Neste contexto, reavaliamos o papel dos últimos caçadores-recolectores dos concheiros do Tejo e do Sado, cuja complexidade social e potencial demográfico permite justificar o extraordinário investimento que subjaz à construção destes monumentos.
Palavras-chave: Recintos Megalíticos; Cronologias; Processo de Neolitização; Ùltimos caçadores-recolectores

INTRODUCTION

In Alentejo, as well as in Algarve, menhirs and groups of menhirs are systematically associated with Early Neolithic materials (Calado, 2004), an association which now and then is confirmed by radiometric methods (Gomes, 1994; Oliveira, 1997).

These early dates imply, among other aspects, some precocity in the start of the megalithic monumentality. The funerary monuments, which are the best known and the most common type of megalithic structures, seem to be, in general terms, a much later phenomenon. As in Brittany, the reuse of menhirs in dolmens is one of the most unavoidable and eloquent evidences of this "genealogy" (Cassen *et al.*, 2000).

Moreover, the striking parallels between the menhirs of Alentejo and Brittany (Scarre, 1998; Cassen *et al.*, 2000; Calado, 2002), especially the horse-shoe plans of the enclosures and the iconography of the standing stones, recall, in a very suggestive way, the strong analogies between the funerary shell-middens of the Breton shoreline and the Tejo-Sado estuary (Roche, 1962; Arnaud, 1987; Marchand, 2001), opening new avenues in the understanding of the complex dynamics of the Western European neolithization.

In both areas, the earliest monuments are, in our opinion, the result of the absorption of the Neolithic way of life (with or without colonization) by the indigenous late Mesolithic communities (Calado, 2004); pottery and

domesticates are likely to have been imported from the East, but megaliths, absent out of the Atlantic coast, seem to be a development, in a ambiance of change, of indigenous ideas and practices.

Fontaínhas was first published, in the mid-seventies, by a team of geologists working on the geological map of the area of Pavia (Zbyszewski *et al.*, 1977).

However, that work was limited to the location and description of the monument, in parallel with a quite precise plan: no artefacts have been reported, and the same can be said about the two menhirs laying outside the enclosure, which were found in the course of field-walking in the area only a few years ago (Calado, 2004).

Five of the six stones of the enclosure had still their base stuck in the respective socket, though showing different angles of inclination; the central menhir was actually broken in two pieces, but with the base rooted in its original emplacement. The two eccentric menhirs (some 10 m and 70 m apart, respectively) were lying with a slight inclination suggesting, before excavation, that the bases would still be in their original position.

The megalithic enclosure of Fontaínhas is part of a complex of monuments, sharing some general features, and apparently concentrated inside the boundaries of Central Alentejo, with (until now) only two exceptions in the vicinity: Torrão (Elvas) and, very close to Fontaínhas, the Alminho enclosure (Ponte de Sor).

Fig. 8.1. Fontaínhas megalithic enclosure in the seventies (photo Marciano da Silva)

It is clear from the distribution map, that the centre of the phenomenon is located in the surroundings of Évora, the heart of Central Alentejo, where the monuments are bigger, more concentrated, and interwoven with a dense network of Early Neolithic settlements (Calado e Rocha, 1996).

The most common characteristics of the Central Alentejan megalithic enclosures are the horse-shoe shape of the plans (the best-preserved example is Vale d'El Rei, also in Pavia county), the orientation of the open side (to the East), the inclination of the ground (to the East), as well as the ovoid general silhouette of the menhirs.

Other features, also quite common, are the presence of at least one larger standing stone inside the western part of the enclosure, or the motifs carved on some menhirs (mostly crooks, crescents, trapezes and circles, following this order). It is also quite frequent that the enclosures show more massive stones on their western side, suggesting an intentional gradation of size. This same feature has been observed and underlined in most known Breton alignments (Le Roux, 2003; Giot, 1992).

THE EXCAVATION OF THE SITE

Fontaínhas was excavated in the summer of 2005, and partially restored one year later.

The objectives of the excavation were basically the determination of the remaining sockets, in order to allow a proper restoration, and the recovery of artefacts, and eventually ecofacts, in context, in order to collect information about the building and the further use of the monument.

The excavation area has been, attending to the usual financial limitations, organized in order to include only the surviving menhirs: in the enclosure (Sector 1), and around each one of the two menhirs, outside that main group (Sectors 2 and 3).

The excavation was driven by natural levels, with the tri-dimensional register of some particular occurrences.

Most of the menhirs in the enclosure had well-preserved sockets, structured with medium size granite stones, except for menhir 2, with only two stones in the socket (though it was in an almost vertical position) and the central menhir (menhir 1), without stones in the socket (but also with the basal part still quite vertical). In both cases, the logical conclusion was that the structures had been removed by taphonomic phenomena, such as the eventual reuse of the site in Roman times or farming activities until the present.

The socket of the more horizontal one (menhir 6) was sufficiently defined, with some stones inside, as well as a new socket, between menhir 5 and menhir 6, without surviving menhir, but quite well preserved.

It is possible that, outside of the excavated trench, there are still other remains of surviving sockets, whose menhirs might have been taken, probably in recent times, for the building of the existing farm-houses in the Fontaínhas area.

Concerning the two outsiders (menhirs 7 and 8), we can say that both of them were demonstrated to be in their original place. Menhir 7, the more distant, still had its base inside the original socket, with a strong structure of medium size stones, the majority of them being, in fact, reused quern stones.

8.2. The monument during the 2005 excavation. The base of menhir 1 is still inside the socket, as well as menhirs 2 and 3; menhirs 4, 5 and 6 have been removed to allow the excavation of the respective implantation structures

The reuse of quern stones has also been observed, on a considerable extension, in the sockets of menhirs 3, 4 and 5.

The menhir 8, the smallest of all, had no stones remaining in the socket, though its inclined position, taking into account the preservation of the others, seems to indicate that it was leaning in its original place.

The stratigraphy outside the sockets proved to be generally disturbed, either by natural causes or by agricultural practices. In fact, the sandy bedrock was only some 30-40 cm deep.

Underneath the fallen part of the broken central menhir, on the contrary, we found a shallow pit, with darker soil. It is probably of Roman age, if we take in account three roman coins and some wheel-made uncharacteristic sherds found in and around it.

All over the excavated area, until the bottom of the levels, many fragments of hand-made pottery (some of them decorated) and plenty of flint artefacts (mostly bladelets, flakes and nuclei, but also two trapezes and one thick chert blade) have been recovered; this material was mixed with modern materials, mostly in the upper levels.

Close to the surface of the sandy bed-rock, two limited clusters of early Neolithic sherds seem to imply a lesser stratigraphic perturbation in the lower parts of the deposits.

Among the ceramic sherds, two carinated bowls have been registered, revealing, together with the chert blade, a Late Neolithic episode, eventually related with the use of the monument; the same continuity of use has been identified in other Alentejan megalithic enclosures and menhirs, such as Cuncos, Pedra Longa or Perdigões (Gomes, 1986; 1994).

THE BEND OF THE RAIA

In parallel with the excavation, the study of the monument included intense field-walking in the surroundings, with the objective of establishing the archaeological context of the monument. This one is situated close to the northern limit of the sandy, flat, arid and undifferentiated landscape – tertiary deposits – which extends to the South and to the West, not far from the first outcrops of granitoid rocks which are the hallmark of the Central Alentejan landscapes.

The river Raia, a subsidiary of the left bank of the Tejo, seems to be the most important natural feature in the area of the monument. In economic terms, its large flat valley, with alluvial deposits, still supports rich farming activity.

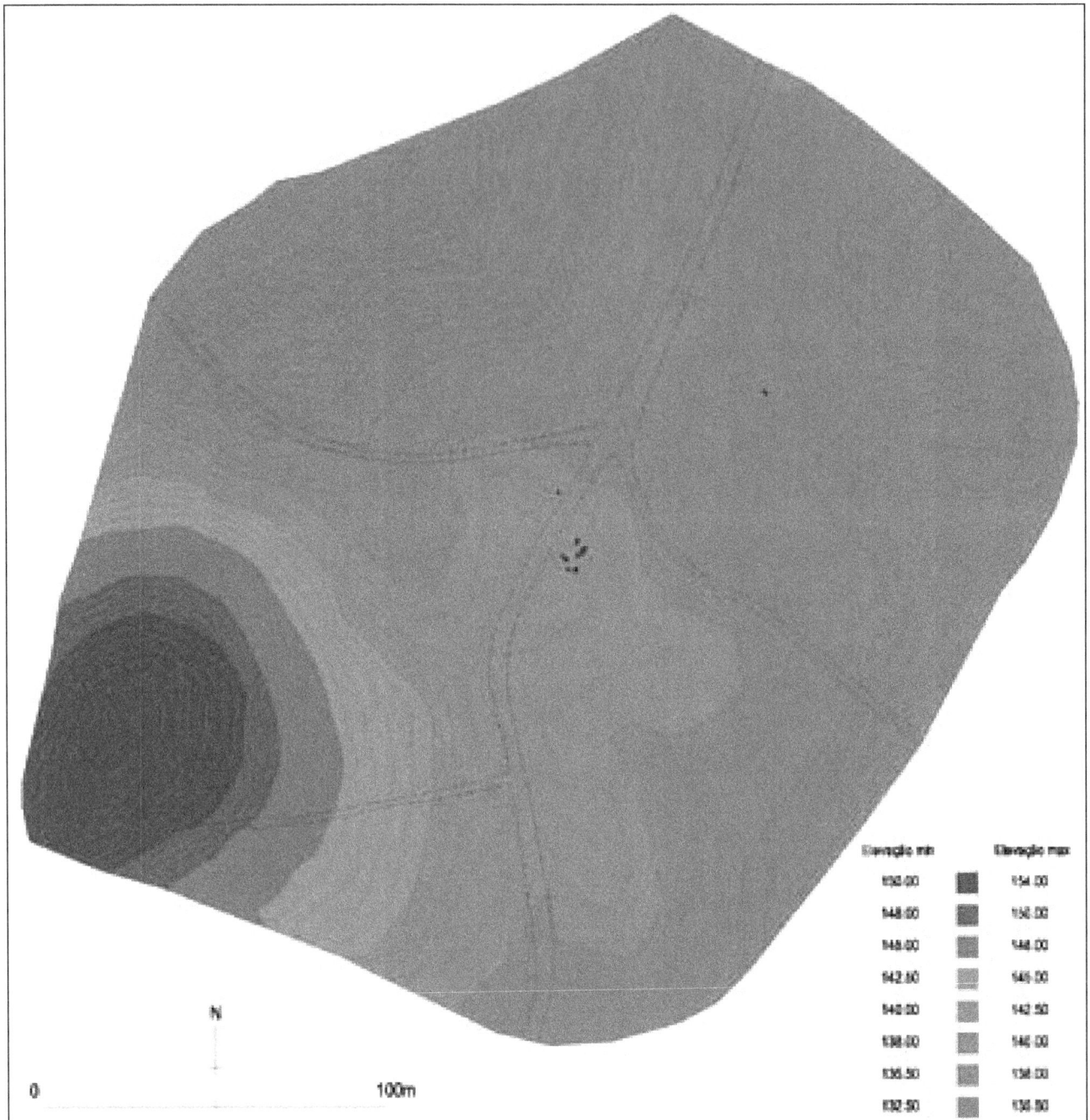

8.3. Plan of the area around the monument of Fontainhas

It has been in the banks of the river that we found the most expressive prehistoric settlements, broadly contemporaneous with the menhirs, apparently spanning from the Late Mesolithic to the Chalcolithic.

In this area, the Raia follows an accentuated bend, and the Fontaínhas enclosure seems to be directly connected, in a North-South alignment, with that conspicuous feature of the landscape.

This fact has already been observed in some important prehistoric cultural sites in Atlantic Europe, apparently articulated with bends of rivers: that is the case, for

example, with Stonehenge in the South of England, or with the Bru na Boyne monuments in Ireland.

In Central Alentejo, the same kind of landscape features appears to have been the focus for the most important rock art concentrations: Moinho da Volta and Retorta, in the Alqueva Dam Rock Art Complex (Calado, 2003).

On the other hand, it is quite well established that the careful and apparently meaningful choice of the emplacement of the other megalithic enclosures, in Central Alentejo, took into account aspects such as the hydrographical ridges and the skyline, possibly

8.4. Menhir 8, after the restoration

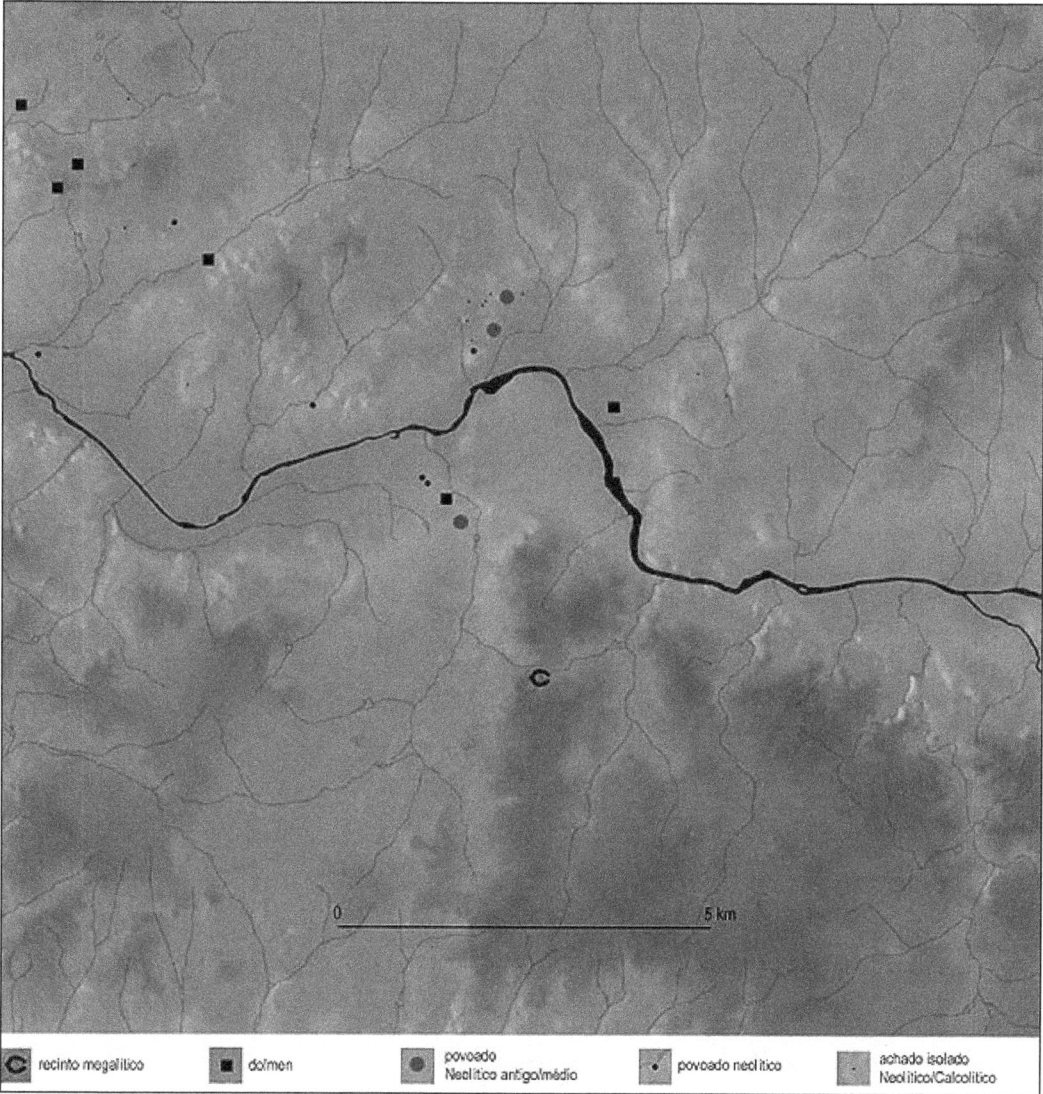

8.5. The area around the megalithic enclosures of Fontainhas

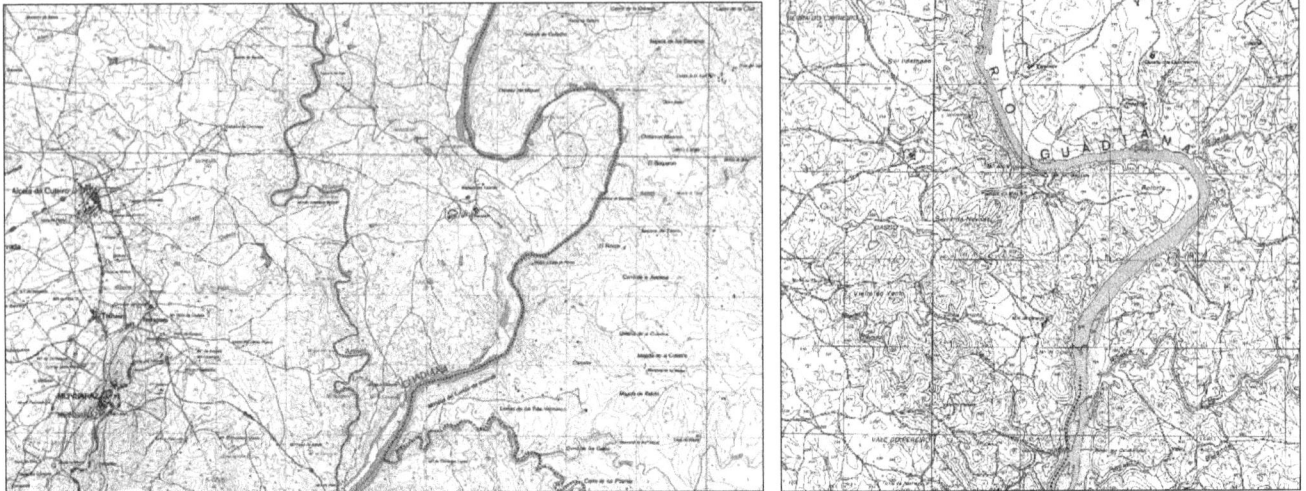

8.6. The main areas with rock art in the Alqueva complex; 1: Moinho da Volta; 2: Retorta

overlapped by significant astronomical directions (Alvim, 2006).

THE SETTLEMENTS

The study of the area, between the enclosure and the bend of the river, did actually reveal a Mesolithic/Neolithic settlement in a suggestively close articulation with the megalithic monument.

That site, Barroca 1, occupies a large platform with around 8 ha., corresponding to a quaternary terrace, slightly elevated above the level of the river and the alluvial plain next to it. In Barroca 1, a set of 24 test pits, distributed along the settlement area, showed a Middle Neolithic occupation, with post-holes, circular stone lined combustion structures, storage pits with the walls covered by burned clay, together with pottery sherds (mostly undecorated; the decorated sherds are reduced to a couple of exemplars with parallel incised lines and one rim with a single incised line below it), and a large quantity of flint artefacts, namely bladelets, cores and geometric microliths (crescents, trapezes and, above all, triangles).

This association of Middle Neolithic pottery with what seems to be a coherent Mesolithic assemblage, is not yet fully understood, and needs further excavation work. The fact that the same basic association was observed along all the area of the site, does not support the hypothesis of two superimposed occupations, separated in time.

As a reliable alternative, we could be dealing with a Mesolithic community which survived, without too many changes, until the middle of the fifth millennium B.C. and that started its process of neolithization when, around it, other communities had already been farmers and/or shepherds for several centuries.

But the study of the area did also cross the river Raia, to the opposite bank; there, we have identified, close to the limits of the alluvial plain, another Early Neolithic settlement (Chaminé 3), with incised and impressed ware (namely cardial), some flint waste, but, for the moment, no microliths at all.

With which one of them (Barroca 1 or Chaminé 3) should we relate the building of the megalithic enclosure of Fontaínhas?

It is early for a definitive answer: dating the Mesolithic occupation of Barroca 1 will, of course, be very useful, and we cannot absolutely exclude the last (and eventually late) hunter gatherers, as the ultimate authors of the monument.

But the materials found in the excavation of Fontaínhas – though not eliminating, in a definitive way, the Mesolithic hypothesis – can favour the Early Neolithic occupation as the most plausible: the two trapezes – larger that those found on Barroca 1- and, particularly, the decorated pottery could belong to the first uses of the enclosure.

A Neolithic date for the construction of the enclosure is strongly suggested by the massive reuse of quern stones inside the sockets of the menhirs. This practice, known in a smaller scale from other excavated megalithic enclosures (Portela de Mogos and Vale Maria do Meio), has been often observed inside the structures of dolmenic monuments (Oliveira, 1998).

DISCUSSION

The assessment of the beginning of monumentality as an event overlapping the Mesolithic-Neolithic transition, is common place in northern parts of Europe.

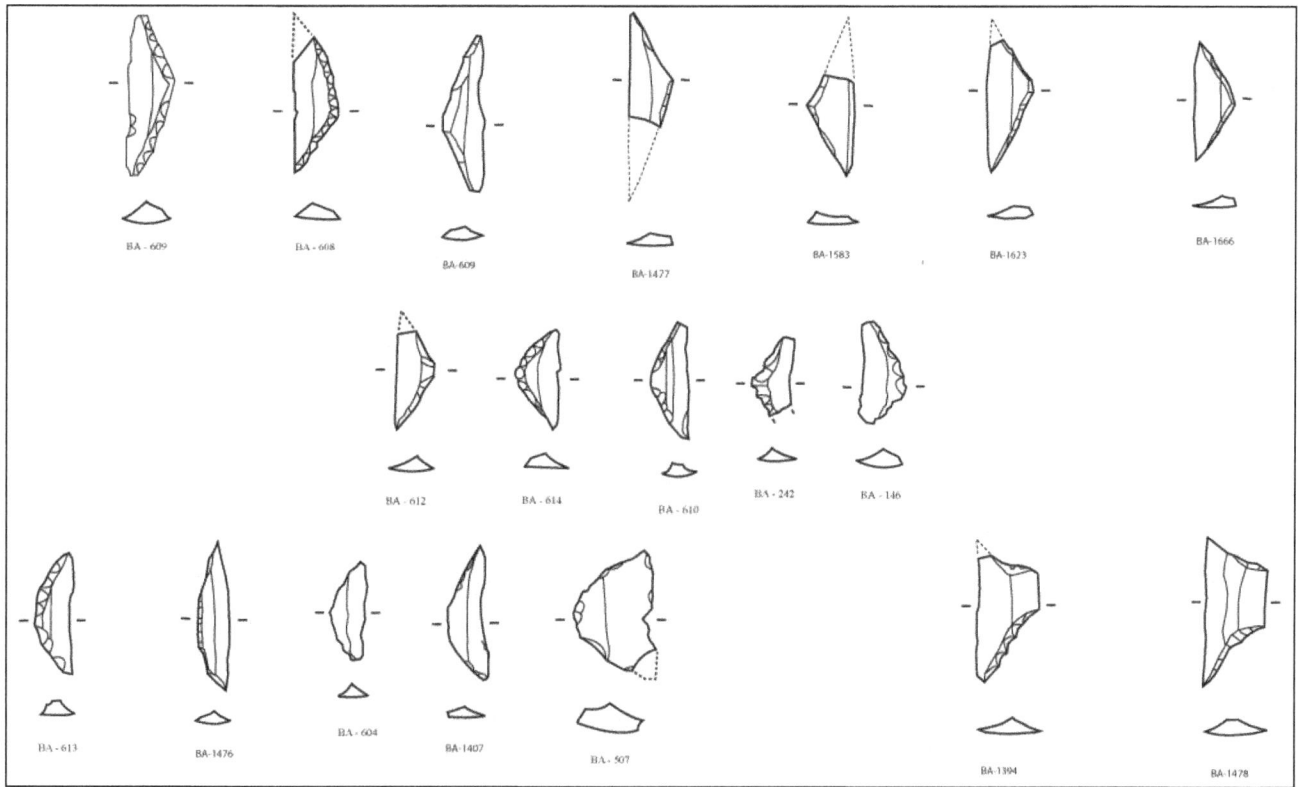

8.7. Geometric microliths from Barroca 1

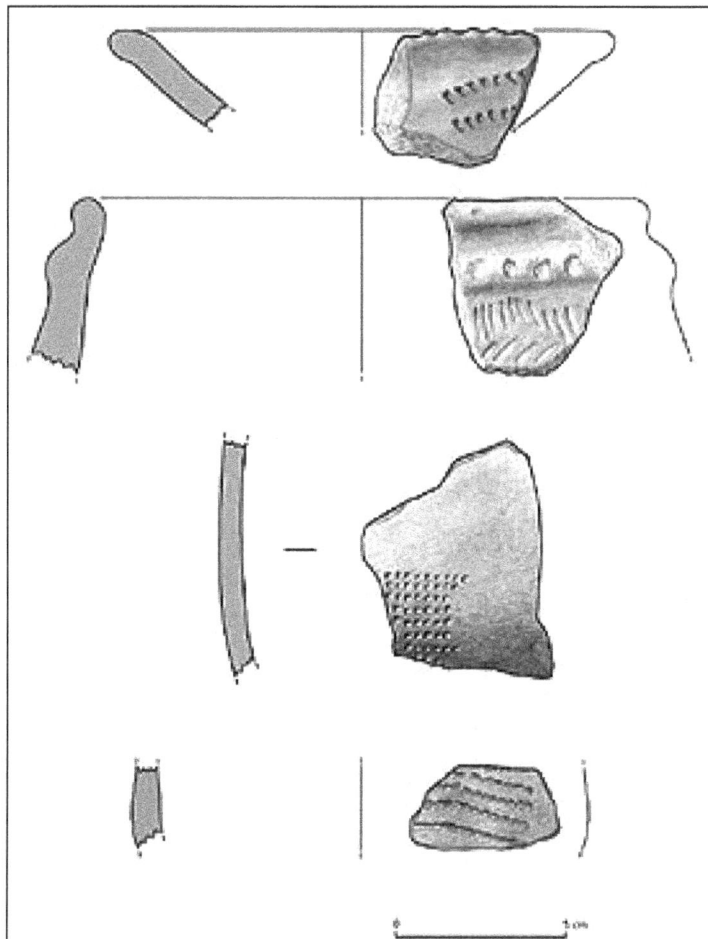

8.8. Pottery from the Chaminé 3 settlement

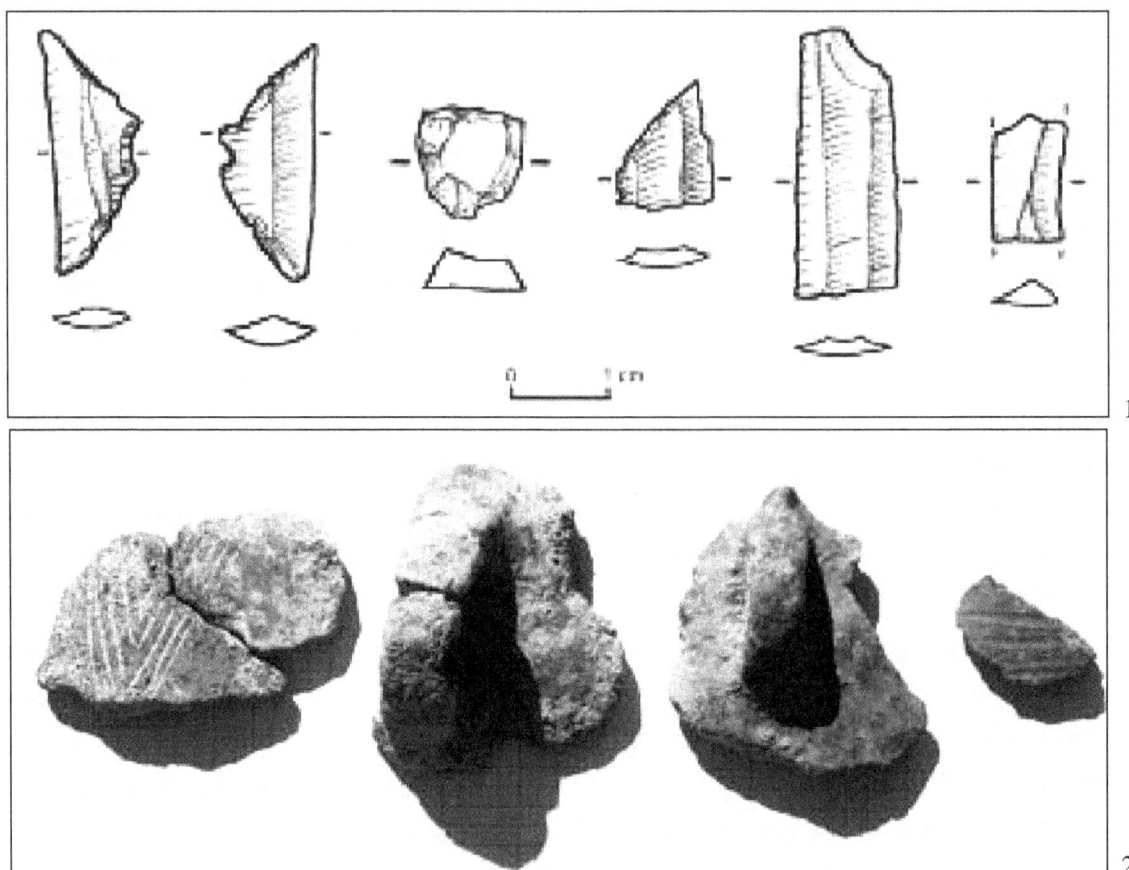

8.9. Lithics (1) and pottery (2) from the excavation of Fontainhas

The misleading Portuguese chronology for the menhirs, accepted, without questioning, until the nineties, created a "Berlin wall" in Neolithic studies, with monuments and settlements (because necropolis are still virtually absent) on each side of the barrier.

Early Neolithic societies, at least in Central Alentejo, need now to be conceived as megalith builders, and this requires corresponding answers on the economical, social, or ideological level.

In this last aspect, which, from the viewpoint of the menhirs, is the most relevant, the neolithization of Central Alentejo is not only receiving ideas from somewhere in the East (Levant, Andalucia) but creating new ideas, or at least, new symbols, on a new scale, to express them. The ideological sources for this particular kind of monumentality seem to exist in the Mesolithic traditions, as exemplified by ritual sites like Moita do Sebastião (Tejo) or Vale de Romeiras (Sado), with post-holes or remnants showing, respectively, the symbolic use of the semi-circular/horse-shoe shaped layout (Roche, 1962; Arnaud, 1999).

On the other hand, the similarities between the Alentejan and the Breton menhirs support another direction of relations, rooted in the Late Mesolithic societies, but still alive during the transition process and eventually beyond.

In a regional perspective, it is important to relate the enclosure of Fontaínhas with the other similar monuments known in the region: the similarities and the differences may result of the crossing of factors as time, geography and the particular historic contingences.

The discovery of Early and Middle Neolithic settlements, as well as a probable Mesolithic occupation, in the vicinity of Fontaínhas, and in a close spatial relationship with it, reinforces the chronology of the monument, giving a very suggestive archaeological context, somewhere around the Mesolithic-Neolithic transition.

This presence, in such an inland context, of Mesolithic evidences gives also some support to reopen the file of the chronological sequence of megalithic enclosures in Central Alentejo. Did that sequence start with the biggest monuments of the core area (Almendres, Portela de Mogos and Vale Maria do Meio), as argued in previous works? Or, on the contrary, did it start with the smaller monuments of the periphery, such as, for instance, Fontaínhas, or, not so far from here, Alminho (Deus, 2002; Angelucci and Deus, 2006), where the same chrono-cultural ambience is also being explored?

Even if no definitive answer can be given to this and other questions, Fontaínhas and its context are a new example of how studying a megalithic monument can ultimately

68

deal with the issue of the Mesolithic-Neolithic transition in Central Alentejo.

References

ALVIM, P. (2006) – Menires, paisagem, paisagens: os Almendres e a Serra do Monfurado. (www.crook-scape.org)

ANGELUCCI, D.; DEUS, M. (2006) – Geomorfologia e ocupação pré-histórica no baixo curso do rio Sor: primeiras observações geoarqueológicas. Revista Portuguesa de Arqueologia. Lisboa: IPA, P. 5-26.

ARNAUD, J. (1987) – Os Concheiros Mesolíticos dos Vales do Tejo e Sado. Semelhanças e diferenças. Arqueologia . Porto. 15, p. 53-64.

ARNAUD, J. (1999) – Os concheiros mesolíticos do vale do Sado e a exploração dos recursos estuarinos (nos tempos pré-históricos e na actualidade). Actas do Encontro sobre Arqueologia da Arrábida. Lisboa: IPA.

BUENO RAMÍREZ, P.; BALBÍN BEHRMANN, R. (2003) – Grafias y territórios megalíticos en Extremadura. Muita gente poucas antas? Origens, espaços e contextos do Megalitismo. Actas do II Colóquio Internacional sobre Megalitismo. Lisboa: IPA, p. 407-448.

CALADO, M. (2001) – Da serra d'Ossa ao Guadiana: um estudo de pré-história regional. Trabalhos de Arqueo-logia, 19. Lisboa: IPA.

CALADO, M. (2003) – Entre o Céu e a Terra. Menires e Arte rupestre no Alentejo Central. In CALADO, M. (Ed.) – Sinais de Pedra. Évora: Fundação Eugénio de Almeida.

CALADO, M. (2004) – Menires do Alentejo Central: génese e evolução da paisagem megalítica regional. Lisboa: Faculdade de Letras da Universidade de Lisboa (Tese de doutoramento policopiada) (www.crookscape.org).

CALADO, M.; ROCHA, L. (1996) – Neolitização do Alentejo Interior: os casos de Pavia e Évora. Actas do I Congrés del Neolític a la Península Ibèrica. Gavà. II, p. 673-682.

CALADO, M.; SARANTOPOULOS, P. (1996) – O Cromeleque de Vale Maria do Meio (Évora, Portugal): contexto arqueológico e geográfico. Actas do I Congrés del Neolític a la Península Ibèrica. Gavà. II, p. 493-504.

CARVALHO, A.F. (1998) – O Abrigo da Pena d'Água (Rexaldia, Torres Novas): resultados dos trabalhos de 1992-1997. Revista Portuguesa de Arqueologia, 2, p. 39-79.

CARVALHO, A.F. (2003) – O Neolítico antigo no Arrife da Serra d'Aire. Um case-study da neolitização da Média e Alta Estremadura. In GONÇALVES, V.S. (ed.) – Muita gente poucas antas? Origens, espaços e contextos do Megalitismo. Actas do II Colóquio

Internacional sobre Megalitismo. Lisboa: IPA, p. 135-154.

CASSEN, S.; BOUJOT, C.; VAQUERO-LASTRES, J. (2000) – Eléments d'architecture. Exploration d'un tertre funéraire à Lannec er Gadouer (Erdeven, Morbihan). Constructions et reconstructions dans le Néolitique morbihonnais. Propositions pour une lecture symbolique. Chauvigny: Association des Publications Chauvignoises.

CERRILLO, E.; PRADA, A.; GONZALEZ, A.; HERAS, F. (2002) – La secuencia cultural de las primeras sociedades productoras en Extremadura: una datación absoluta del yacimiento de Los Barruecos (Malpartida de Cáceres, Cáceres). Trabajos de Prehistoria. Madrid, 59: 2, p. 101-111.

DEUS, M. (2002) – Povoamento Neolítico e Calcolítico na região de Montargil. Lisboa: Faculdade de Letras da Universidade de Lisboa (tese fotocopiada).

DINIZ, M. (2003) – O sítio da Valada do Mato (Évora). Aspectos da neolitização no Interior Sul de Portugal. Lisboa: Faculdade de Letras da Universidade de Lisboa (tese de Doutoramento policopiada).

DINIZ, M.; CALADO, M. (1997) – O povoado neolítico da Valada do Mato (Évora, Portugal) e as origens do megalitismo alentejano. In BALBÍN, R.; BUENO, P. – Actas do II Congreso de Arqueologia Peninsular. TII-Neolítico, Calcolítico y Bronce. Zamora: Fundación Rei Afonso Henriques, p. 23-32.

FERREIRA, A. (2006) – O Povoado Neolítico de Patalim. Lisboa: Faculdade de Letras da Universidade de Lisboa (Tese de mestrado policopiada).

FOWLER, C.; CUMMINGS, V. (2003) – Places Of Transformation: Building Monuments From Water And Stone In The Neolithic Of The Irish Sea Journal of the Royal Anthropological Institute 9 (1), 1–20.

GIOT, P.-R. (1988) – Stones in the Landscape of Brittany. In RUGGLES, C. (ed.) – Records in Stone. Cambridge: Cambridge University Press, p.319-324.

GIOT, P.-R. (1992) – Les alignements de Carnac. Rennes: Éd. Ouest-France.

GOMES, M.V. (1986) – O cromeleque da Herdade de Cuncos (Montemor-o-Novo, Évora). Almansor. 4, p. 7-42.

GOMES, M.V. (1994) – Menires e cromeleques no complexo cultural megalítico português – trabalhos recentes e estado da questão. Actas do Seminário "O Megalitismo no Centro de Portugal". Viseu, p. 317-342.

GONÇALVES, V.S. (2002a) – Duas áreas de inesperado avanço sobre a vida e a morte das antigas sociedades camponesas do Guadiana médio – a mega-operação do Alqueva, um balanço dos blocos 3 e 6 em fins de 2002. Al-Madan, IIª série, 11, p. 99-108.

GONÇALVES, V.S. (2002b) – Lugares de povoamento das antigas sociedades camponesas entre o Guadiana e a Ribeira do Álamo (Reguengos de Monsaraz): um ponto da situação em inícios de 2002. Revista Portuguesa de Arqueologia. Lisboa, 5: 2, p. 163-189.

GONÇALVES, V.S. (2003) – Comer em Reguengos, no Neolítico. As estruturas de combustão da Área 3 de Xarez 12. In GONÇALVES, V.S. (ed.) – Muita gente poucas antas? Origens, espaços e contextos do Megalitismo. Actas do II Colóquio Internacional sobre Megalitismo. Lisboa: IPA, p. 81-99.

LE ROUX, C.-T. (2003) – Les menhirs d'Armorique et leur place dans la vie des hommes du Néolithique. Muita gente poucas antas? Origens, espaços e contextos do Megalitismo. Actas do II Colóquio Internacional sobre Megalitismo. Lisboa: IPA, p. 339-349.

MARCHAND, G. (2001) – La néolitisation de l'Europe atlantique: mutations des systèmes techniques en France et au Portugal. Annales de la Fondation Fyssen, 16, p. 115-124.

OLIVEIRA, J. (1997) – Datas absolutas de monumentos megalíticos da Bacia Hidrográfica do Rio Sever. In BALBÍN, R.; BUENO, P. – Actas do II Congreso de Arqueologia Peninsular. TII-Neolítico, Calcolítico y Bronce. Zamora: Fundación Rei Afonso Henriques, p. 229-239.

OLIVEIRA, J. (1998) – Monumentos Megalíticos da Bacia Hidrográfica do Rio Sever. Lisboa: Ed. Colibri.

ROCHA, L. (2005) – Origens do megalitismo funerário no Alentejo Central: a contribuição de Manuel Heleno. Lisboa: Faculdade de Letras da Universidade de Lisboa (Tese de Doutoramento policopiada).

ROCHE, J. (1972) – Le gisement mésolithique de Moita do Sebastião, Muge, Portugal-Archéologie. Vol. I. Lisboa: Direcção-Geral dos Assuntos Culturais.

SANTOS, M.F. (1971) – A Cerâmica Cardial da Gruta do Escoural. Actas do II Congresso Nacional de Arqueologia. Lisboa: AAP, 1, p. 93-95.

SCARRE, C. (1998) – Exploring Prehistoric Europe. Oxford: Oxford University Press.

SOARES, J.; SILVA, C.T. (1992) – Para o conhecimento dos povoados do megalitismo de Reguengos. Setúbal Arqueológica. Setúbal. IX-X, p. 37-88.

SOARES, J.; SILVA, C.T. (2000a) – Capturar a mudança na pré-história recente do Sul de Portugal. Actas do 3º Congresso de Arqueologia Peninsular. Porto: Adecap, vol. IV, p. 213-224.

SOARES, J.; SILVA, C.T. (2000b) – Protomegalitismo no Sul de Portugal: inauguração das paisagens megalíticas. In Gonçalves, V.S. (ed.) Muitas Antas, Pouca Gente?- Actas do Colóquio Internacional sobre Megalitismo. Lisboa: IPA, 117-134.

SOARES, J.; SILVA, C.T. (2003) – A transição para o Neolítico na costa sudoeste portuguesa. In Gonçalves, V.S., (ed.) Muita gente poucas antas? Origens, espaços e contextos do Megalitismo. Actas do II Colóquio Internacional sobre Megalitismo. Lisboa: IPA, p. 45-56.

ZBYSZEWSKI, G.; FERREIRA, O. V.; REYNOLDS de SOUSA, H.; NORTH, C.T.; LEITÃO, M. (1977a) – Nouvelles découvertes de Cromelechs et de Menhirs au Portugal. CSGP. Lisboa. LXI, p. 63-73.

CASTELO BELINHO (ALGARVE, PORTUGAL) AND THE FIRST SOUTHWEST IBERIAN VILLAGES

Mário VARELA GOMES

Abstract: The excavation of an Islamic fortress named Castelo Belinho led to the identification and exploration of the first Extreme Southwest Iberian Neolithic village. Longhouses, constructed with wooden posts identified by holes in the ground, grain storage pits, hearths, cobbled floors and ritual and funerary pits were the architectural elements found, all presenting a large variety of forms.
Four ^{14}C analyses indicate a middle of the 5th millennium settlement. The material culture is composed of knapped flint and pecked/polished stone artefacts, pottery and shell adornments.
Castelo Belinho's population was completely neolithized, practising a successful food production economy based on agriculture and animal husbandry, primarily goats but also sheep.
The settlement strategy shows complete sedentariness; located on high ground with some natural defences, from where a vast area of territory could be controlled, surrounded by productive agricultural lands and pastures though not far from the ocean, a distance an individual could travel in a day. The presence of rectangular longhouses, ritual pits and inhumation pits is an archaeological novelty in the area. They reflect significant social differences and hierarchy, especially through the house dimensions and through the commodities placed with the deceased.
Key-words: Late Early Neolithic, Early Middle Neolithic, longhouse, storage pit, pit grave

Resumo: A escavação da fortaleza islâmica denominada Castelo Belinho conduziu à identificação e investigação da primeira aldeia neolítica do Extremo Sudoeste da Península Ibérica.
Casas longas, edificadas com postes de madeira, detectados através de buracos abertos no solo, silos, estruturas de combustão, empedrados e fossas rituais ou funerárias, constituem os elementos arquitectónicos encontrados, apresentando todos eles largo polimorfismo.
Quatro análises pelo método do radiocarbono indicam tratar-se de assentamento de meados do V milénio A.C. A cultura material é constituída por artefactos de pedra lascada ou picotada/polida, cerâmicas e adornos de concha.
A população do Castelo Belinho encontrava-se plenamente neolitizada, praticando economia de produção de alimentos, com sucesso, baseada na agricultura e na pastorícia, sobretudo de caprinos mas também de ovinos.
A estratégia de ocupação mostra perfeita sedentarização, localizando-se em lugar elevado, com algumas defesas naturais, de onde se podia controlar visualmente vasta área, envolvida por terras agrícolas muito produtivas e pastos, não muito longe do Oceano, onde se podia ir e voltar no mesmo dia.
A presença de casas rectangulares, de fossas rituais ou para inumação, e de desenvolvida economia de produção de alimentos, constituíram, então, inovações na região. Estes testemunhos reflectem diferenças sociais e hierarquização significativas, designadamente através das dimensões das casas e devido aos espólios que acompanhavam os mortos.
Palavras-Chave: Final do Neolítico antigo; Início do Neolítico médio; Casas longas; silos; fossas funerárias

IDENTIFICATION, ARCHAEOLOGICAL DIGGINGS AND ISSUES

The project to study and evaluate the ruins of a small earth wall (*pisé*) Islamic fortress named Castelo Belinho, located in the extreme Iberian Southwest, just 6 kilometres from the southern shore, led to the unexpected discovery and complete archaeological excavation of a village from Early Neolithic times.

The archaeological work, entirely funded by Imoreguengo, the site owner, took place during the summers of 2004 and 2005, and a monographic study is currently being undertaken.

Diverse negative structure types were identified, namely numerous aligned postholes dug in the bedrock and shaping spaces such as longhouses, grain storage pits or silos for food storage, depositional pits and combustion pits or hearths, as well as shallow and deep inhumation pits. We also found cobbled floors associated to fireplaces. A large variety of artefacts were recovered as well as carbonised plants and malacological and mammalogical faunal remains. These were the result of daily human activities and cognitive life practices, and were recovered in ritual and symbolic depositions and even graves.

This evidence indicates Late Early Neolithic or the transition period to the Early Middle Neolithic, which four radiocarbon calibrated analyses dated to the middle of the 5th millennium BC. The average of these dates is exactly 4500 BC.

Contrary to available archaeological data, until the discovery and excavation of the Castelo Belinho Neolithic village, the Southern Portuguese Early Plain Neolithic (*ca* 5600-5000 BC), Late Early Neolithic (*ca* 5000-4500 BC), or even Early Middle Neolithic settlements occupied areas on the plains close to important waterways or near the seashore, generally with easy to work sandy soils, without any natural or artificial defences. They provide evidence of sparse occupation, though they are sometimes extensive covering several hectares, but few habitational structures remain. This makes it impossible to recognize the shape of the houses, and there are no nearby graves or other negative ritual structures. Nevertheless, standing stones have been identified in some settlements.

SETTLEMENT STRATEGY

The Castelo Belinho Neolithic village, the first southern Portuguese site where the spatial organization permits us

Fig.9.1. Castelo Belinho village location and plan of identified structures
(○ storage, foundational and depositional pits; ⊗ cobbled floors; ⊘ pit graves; ● postholes)

to call it such, is located on the southern side of a long Miocenic limestone rock hill, bordered to the north by the steep slopes of the Monchique mountain and to the south by the plains near the sea. The eastern side is defended

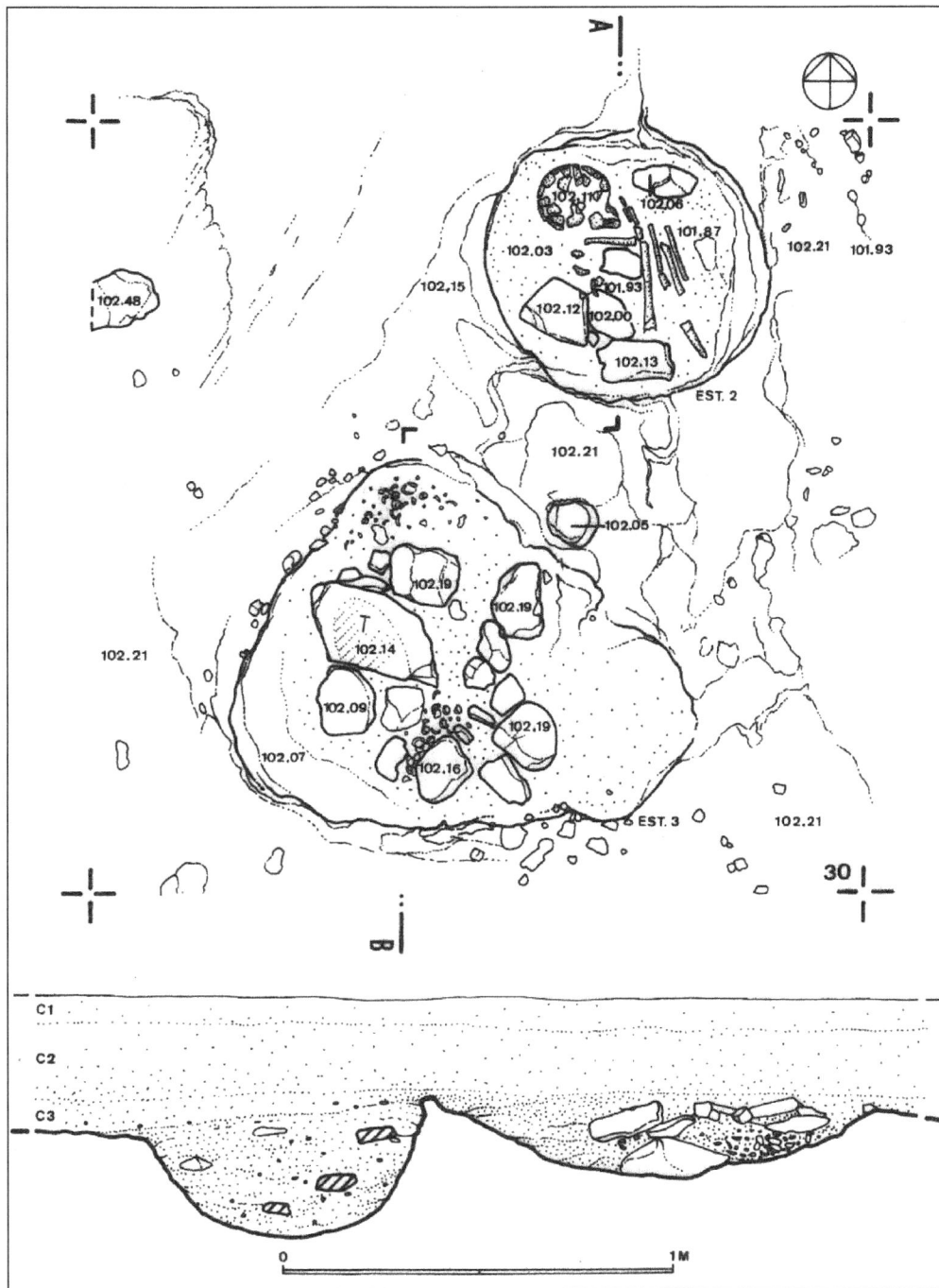

Fig. 9.2. Castelo Belinho. Structures 2 (grave) and 3 (depositional pit)

naturally by steep hillsides and by the valley of the Boina stream.

From this high ground (105 m), a vast area of territory, with the ocean in sight, could be controlled. Access paths, fields of crops, pastures and animal herds, the major economic resources at that time, were all in view. The journey to the River Arade estuary, 5 km away south by south-east, could be made by following the Boina stream valley. To reach the sea required a further 4 km walk. To the southwest, it was possible to reach the Torre stream valley and the Atlantic, 6 km away.

HOUSE STRUCTURES

Having identified the postholes, some of which still contained stone wedges, the layout of at least five rectangular modular longhouses, primitively constructed with strong wooden posts and rafters, could be delineated. Note that the possibility of some posts being supported by stone rings should not be ignored.

The best preserved postholes group belonged to a house which was 16 m long by 2,90 m wide. Three lines of post-holes with an east-west orientation and approximately

73

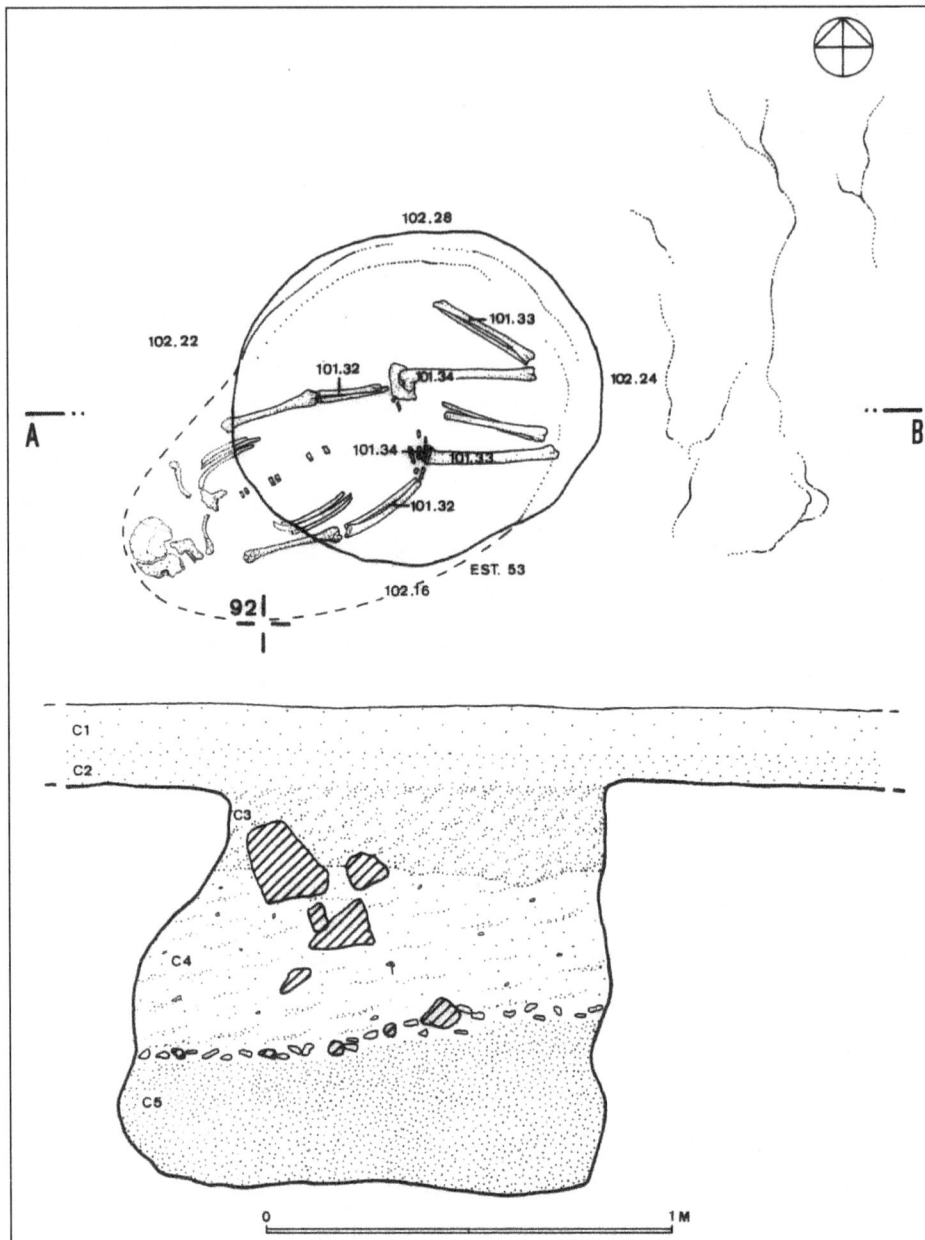

Fig. 9.3. Castelo Belinho. Structure 53 (grave)

1,60 m apart supported the walls and the gable roof, possibly thatched with straw or rushes. The door would be in the centre of the southern façade, permitting maximum sunlight penetration. Inside a cobbled floor was found in the central area.

Another house, 12,40 m long by 2,90 m wide and also oriented east-west, shows no clear evidence of a central post line to support the roof's central ridgepole, so a simple sloping roof must have covered it. This building was superimposed on two depositional pits.

Two other houses showing a more irregular layout and a trapezoidal plan were 7,20 m and 8,30 m long, by 2,90 m and 3,20 m wide, respectively, with three rows of postholes indicating gable roofs. The first house was

oriented north-south whilst the second was located at an oblique angle to the first.

Another trapezoidal-shaped house with a sloping roof was smaller, measuring only 3,60 m long by 2,20 m wide.

The living-area floors of these houses were possibly of beaten earth and no porches or elaborate entrances were detected.

The location of some of the postholes leads us to consider that these structures were rebuilt and enlarged as well as being superimposed. All these aspects relate to the dynamics of the site occupation during the Neolithic which must have lasted less then half a millennium.

Functional areas inside the houses such as storage, sleeping and working/living areas were difficult to recognize owing to the destruction of the archaeological levels.

The house dimensions permit us to calculate that if each individual needed at least 4 m² to live, then the village would have had some 40 to 50 inhabitants.

Four larger postholes were detected in the centre of the settlement, arranged in a semi-circle with a diameter of 2 m. This certainly corresponds to a non-habitable structure, the function of which we have not as yet discovered.

PRODUCTION-RELATED STRUCTURES (HEARTHS, COBBLED FLOORS AND STORAGE PITS)

The various hearths identified were generally small in size, about 0,40 m in diameter, with a subcircular or oval shape, dug in shallow pits. They were filled with thermoclasts (heat-conserving stones) which showed fire marks, burnt earth and sometimes pottery sherds and other materials, notably food remains (bones and sea shells).

Two cobbled floors, one of them 2,40 m long, had been preserved owing to their location in natural rock depressions. They were made of small-size greywacke, syenite and limestone blocks and contained parts of grinding stones and earth. They also presented fire marks.

These structures could have been used for cooking or heating, and they were possibly used for smoking food (fish and meat) to preserve it.

Oval or sack-shaped negative structures, narrower at the top and wider in the middle, dug in the rock, were found filled with earth. They may have been used as storage pits for conserving cereals or dried fruits for the long or middle term.

RITUAL STRUCTURES (FOUNDATIONAL OR DEPOSITIONAL PITS AND GRAVES)

At the bottom of some cylindrical and hemispherical pits, sealed by a series of medium-sized rocks and completely filled with earth, were found grinding stone fragments, powerful but rough polished stone artefacts (axes and adzes) and enormous sherds of bowls and tall pottery containers.

One of these structures, in which the walls and bottom were covered by flagstones, maybe heralded the pre-megalithic tombs from the Middle Neolithic. Another contained burnt earth, manual upper and lower grinding stone fragments and ceramic sherds as well as pieces of skull and the human bones of a man of over 20 years old.

Could this be a sign of ritual cannibalism or an ancestry cult, with circulation of the anatomic parts of the dead?

Negative structures of different shapes, which we believe are also related to ritual depositions, offered burnt earth, grinding stone fragments and flint artefacts, and at the top of one of them were some pottery sherds.

All the graves identified were of the inhumation type and indicate a low standardisation of funerary ritual. Two main categories can be identified: graves in small pits dug in the ground or in natural depressions where the body, located near the surface, was laid in lateral foetal *decubitus*; the others were silo-shaped pits of different sizes, where the body was laid in the aforesaid position in the smaller examples, while in the larger ones, the corpse presented either the same position or dorsal *decubitus* with the legs folded backwards.

In one large grave, a grown adult male of over 35 years old was laid with twenty-two *Glycymeris bimaculata* shell bracelets on his arms (struct. 4), while other individuals, though also buried in large pits, bore no artefacts as grave goods.

ARTEFACTS

The settlement's occupation level revealed knapped flint-work, pecked/polished stone artefacts, pottery and shell adornments.

Among the abundant remains of different colour and origin from knapped flint industries, were identified cores, blades, geometric microliths, denticulated flake fragments (maybe used in sickles or *tribuli*), piercers and blade or flake scrapers. Debris was found indicating flint tool production. This raw material is known along the Algarve coast although some of the types identified were obtained from more distant sources.

The pecked/polished stone artefacts found were grinding stones (querns and handstones), hammers, axes, adzes and gouges, all linked to agricultural work or woodworking technology. Three smaller adzes recorded should be interpreted as votive artefacts, the only tools bearing this classification. In fact, the absence of ritual or ideotechnic artefacts must be noted.

The pottery recipients show a wide variety of shapes and sizes, from small bowls to large spherical vases, some sack-shaped, with an uncommon impressed, incised, plastic or red-painted decoration, but usually combining two or more such techniques.

Glycymeris glycymeris shells were used as pendants, and shell beads and a pin were also found. These reveal one of mankind's most ancient symbolic behaviours which goes back in Europe to at least the Middle Palaeolithic.

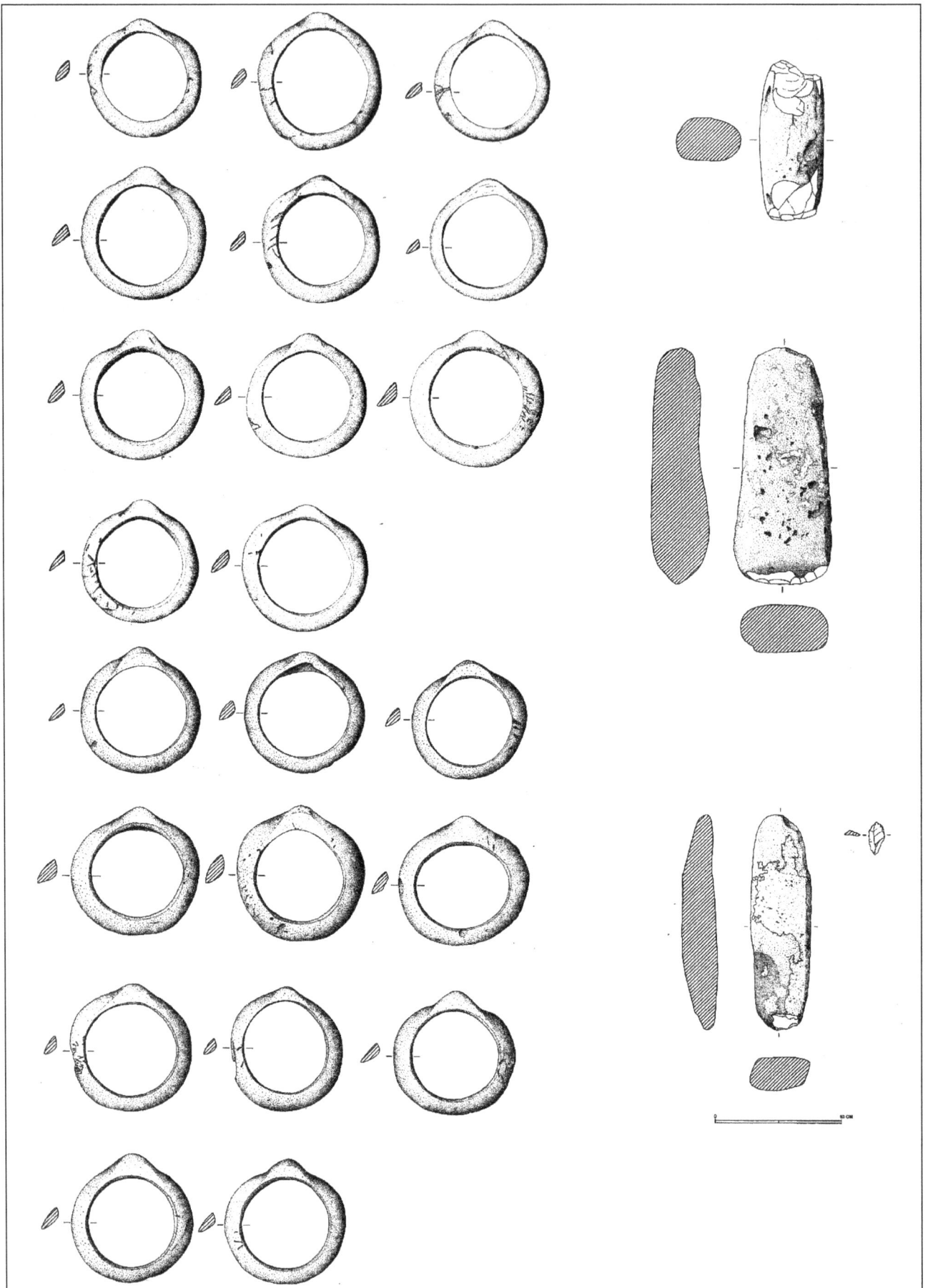

Fig. 9.4. Castelo Belinho. *Glycymeris bimaculata* bracelets and axe (structure 4), axe (structure 26) and an adze (structure 27)

Samples	Lab. Nº	Sample	Age B.P.	Calibrated date (2 *sigma*)
CAST. BEL. EST. 1 (ritual pit)	Sac – 2031	*Venerupis + Mytilus*	5790 ± 70	4364-4046 cal. B.C.
CAST. BEL. EST. 2 (grave)	Beta 199912	Human bones	5500 ± 40	4380-4320 cal. B.C. 4290-4260 cal. B.C.
CAST. BEL. EST. 3 (ritual pit)	Sac – 2030	*Venerupis*	6260 ± 45	4900-4864 cal. B.C. 4855-4598 cal. B.C.
CAST. BEL. EST. 4 (grave)	Beta 199913	Human bones	5720 ±40	4680-4460 cal. B.C.

Radiocarbon dates, traditional and AMS

In the settlement's occupation levels, the distribution of finds occurred mainly around the houses.

CONCLUSIONS

The settlement strategy used for Castelo Belinho - located on high ground with natural defences, a single day's journey to and from the coast, controlling a vast expanse of territory and surrounded by heavy but productive soils - was hitherto unknown for a middle of the 5th millennium permanent long-term settlement. This strategy reveals a new economic, social and ideological model.

The successful food production economy and sedentary life were supported by agriculture and animal husbandry. This is not only revealed by the settlement's location, but also through the enormous quantity of polished stone tools (axes, adzes and gouges), some broken due to intensive labour, which were found along with dozens of grinding stones (handstones and saddle querns), sickle and/or *tribuli* flint blades, pottery containers of considerable size for provisions and grain storage pits. The goat and sheep husbandry is well documented by the quantity of osteological remains recovered. Also recovered, but in smaller quantities, were those of bovines.

The artefacts mentioned and the pottery shapes and decoration were well known from Late Early Neolithic settlements in Western Algarve (Caramujeira and Areias das Almas – Lagoa) that we have investigated and on the southwestern Portuguese coast (Gomes, 1997; Gomes & Cabrita, 1997; Silva & Soares, 1991). The technical, formal and decorative types of ceramic are important factors in cultural and social identity, able to define regionalisms and economic interaction networks.

Another Early Neolithic settlement, located on a small hill near the seashore at Vau (Portimão) about 8 km from Castelo Belinho and identified by us some years ago, was similarly formed by at least two rectangular houses, one of them with a gable roof and measuring 3,60 m long by 3,20 m wide, and the other measuring 5,20 m long by 2,70 m wide. Several pits were also present.

Evidence of another contemporary settlement, also showing negative structures excavated in the bedrock, was identified at Mato Serrão (Lagoa), also near the shore.

Summarizing, the evidence presents an Early Neolithic settlement where free-standing timber buildings associated to graves containing anthropological remains indicate a new habitat concept with a stable social life. Different ritual aspects were also uncovered for the first time in Southern Portugal.

In spite of the great social cohesion and identity shown by the village structure with its longhouses where we can presume the space was shared by several members of a family, the social differentiation, social organization and hierarchy in the village is revealed by the diversity of house areas and by the inhumation rituals, especially given the forms and size of the graves. This differentiation can also be seen through the commodities deposited with the deceased, namely prestige goods. The graves and other depositional pits occupied a communal space among the houses near the living, thus demonstrating social solidarity and a possible Mesolithic inheritance. The storage pits are not associated to specific houses and some of the larger ones could be for communal use, thereby reflecting a strong cooperative lifestyle, perhaps a communitarian model, linking the multi-family householders.

The archaeological data presented here for the first time shows hitherto unknown aspects of Southwest Iberian Prehistory, namely the existence in Early Neolithic times of villages with wooden longhouses built with posts and demonstrating a high level of carpentry skills. These are associated to burial pits contemporary with the ones found in Central Europe. This data contradicts the most recurrent model of the neolithization of the Southwest Iberian Peninsula, developed in the 1970's. Here neolithization was conceived as a reflection of the slow intrusion of the Neolithic package into the last appropriation-based economies, namely in seashore sites where the easy gathering of sea molluscs and other maritime food resources would last until a later date (Silva & Soares, 1991).

However, although presenting few archaeological arguments, for the last few years J. Zilhão (2003) has defended that neolithization developed through colonizing agriculturalist settlers from the Mediterranean, who established themselves in enclaves and interacted with the local population (indigenous foragers). This model does not explain the Castelo Belinho and Vau longhouses, whose typology and village organization seem to have parallels in the longhouse settlements of the *Linienband Keramische Kultur* of Central and Western Europe (*ca* 5500-4500 BC) (Whittle, 1996; Last, 1996).

References

CALADO, D.C., 2000, Poblados con menhirs del Extremo SW Peninsular. Notas para su cronologia e economía. Una aproximación cuantitativa, *Revisra Atlántica-Mediterránea de Prehistoria y Arqueologia Social*, 1, p. 7-27

GOMES, M.V., 1997, Megalitismo do Barlavento Algarvio – Breve síntese, *Setúbal Arqueológica*, 11-12, p. 147-190.

GOMES, M.V. & CABRITA, L.M., 1997, Dois novos povoados neolíticos, com menires, no Barlavento Algarvio, *Setúbal Arqueológica*, 11-12, p. 191-198.

LAST, J., 1996, Neolithic houses – A central European perspective. In: *Neolithic Houses in Northwest Europe and Beyond*, p. 13-26. Oxford: Oxford Books.

SILVA, C.T. & SOARES, J., 1991, *Pré-História da Área de Sines*. Lisboa: Gabinete da Área de Sines.

WHITTLE, A., 1996, Houses in context: Buildings as process. In: *Neolithic Houses in Northwest Europe and Beyond*, p. 13-26. Oxford: Oxbow Books.

ZILHÃO, J., 2003, The Neolithic transition in Portugal and the role of demic diffusion in the spear of agriculture across West Mediterranean Europe. In: *The Widening Harvest. The Neolithic Transition in Europe: Looking Back, Looking Forward*, p. 207-223. Boston: Archaeological Institute of America.